THE ART OF CONTRARY THINKING

D0888315

BY THE SAME AUTHOR

Tape Reading and Market Tactics (New York: Forbes Publishing Company, 1931). Reprints from Fraser Publishing Co., Wells, Vt.

Understanding American Business (New York: The Macmillan Company, 1939).

Forty-eight Million Horses (Electrical Industry) (Philadelphia: J. B. Lippincott Company, 1940).

The Inside Story of the New York Stock Exchange (New York: B. C. Forbes & Sons Publishing Co., Inc., May, 1950).

It Pays To Be Contrary (a pamphlet, 1951, which becomes a part of the present volume).

Neill Letters of Contrary Opinion.

Fraser-Neill Letters of Contrary Opinion, Wells, Vt.

THE ART OF
Contrary Thinking

by

HUMPHREY B. NEILL
(The Vermont Ruminator)

It Pays To Be Contrary

SIXTH AND ENLARGED EDITION

CAXTON PRESS
CALDWELL, IDAHO
2010

First printing, January 1954
Second printing, March 1956
Third printing, January 1960
Fourth printing, July 1963
Fifth printing, August 1967
Sixth printing, September 1971
Seventh printing, December 1976
Eighth printing, July 1980
Ninth printing, August 1985
Tenth printing, December 1992
Eleventh printing, October 2001
Twelfth printing, August 2003
Thirteenth printing, March 2004
Fourteenth printing, April 2007
Fifteenth printing November 2010

6th Edition

ISBN 978-0-870-04110-5

COPYRIGHT 1954, 1956, 1960 AND 1963
THE CAXTON PRINTERS, LTD.
CALDWELL, IDAHO

Cover image: "Thinking at Hell's Gate" ©*Innoxious@flickr*
Cover image adapted via Creative Commons Attribution License 3.0

Lithographed and Bound in the United States of America by
CAXTON PRESS
Caldwell, Idaho 83605
179841

To Contrarians and Libertarians
everywhere. May their numbers
grow!

TABLE OF CONTENTS

INTRODUCTION
by Tim Vanech

Last week I went to Barnes and Noble looking for two new books written on the Great Recession of 2008. Surprisingly, these titles were not available in the store. While the employees at the information desk searched their website inventory (unsuccessfully), I went to double check the business section. Instead of the books I was looking for, which must have been considered too technical for mass consumption, I found several bookcases full of shiny offerings in the "personal finance" space. Out of curiosity, I took a Humphrey B. Neill-like stroll around the entire mega store, trolling for a sense of what was most popular with the crowd. Neill believed that if we could follow the growing fascinations of the crowd, and then ruminate and reflect on opposing, contrary perspectives, that we could develop our own minds more fully and independently—that we could be more creative, get closer to a sense of truth, and have a better understanding of the larger forces operating on us and our position within the world.

As I passed through the store aisles, I scanned tables of new releases, coffee table and travel books, cds, dvds, periodicals, the children's section, and obligatory in-store cafe. At the back of the store next to a narrow, stand-alone bookcase of literary classics, I experienced my epiphany. The best locations at the front of the store, as well as the largest amount of shelf space had all been allocated to books that tell us **how to get rich.**

From my brief, unscientific bookstore browsing, I had confirmed a facile, long-held observation about American culture. We are obsessed with money. More than sex, Hollywood icons, or gossip biographies, star athletes, family dysfunction, recipes, or wellness, it is fear and greed surrounding money that gets us to swipe our credit cards. Despite this national obsession and the accompanying industry that has evolved to profit from it, our skills as a people seem to be weakening when it comes to the acquisition and protection of wealth (exhibit one: the Great Recession of 2008). That must be why we crave books to teach us the basics—the exact steps we need to copy.

And that is just the problem with the approach taken by many of these books. The authors try to share with us the secrets of *others*; how is that rich person's mind wired? They promise to reveal the work of the gurus and masters of money. What do they do that I can't do? Give me a workbook. Give me exercises. I want to know the seven habits, the seven steps, the three pillars of prosperity. Just don't make me think for myself—or about myself. I want to *do* something, *anything*. Give me something to do, so I can be an American money ninja like those tanned shouters on CNBC.

Maybe the problem is that these experts espouse so many ways of enriching themselves, I mean, us, that it becomes overwhelming to choose only one path. One author guarantees success if we buy foreclosure properties. Rich Dad Kiyosaki tells us that being a lifelong employee is the road to financial ruin. Another guru tells us that he has a magic formula for identifying cheap stocks at the push of a few virtual internet buttons, while yet another proffers a methodology utilizing fixed, guaranteed insurance products as the way to *financial independence*—a term that always reminds me of "Depends," those adult diapers. David Bach tells us if we just grind our own cheap, coffee beans and avoid buying lattes at Starbucks, then we can "automatically" become like our rich, unassuming neighbor with the old truck and worn Sears khaki pants who lives like a hermit with his staycations, Costco runs, his Quicken reports, and perfectly integrated, online investment plan. You can almost hear a low toned chant through this aisle of books in praise of dollar cost averaging.

I admit that I am no different in that I am also obsessed with money. I am a money manager by nature and training, and I would bet very few of my friends and clients would argue that I should be doing something else. I am passionate about my work, and hopefully I have gained a bit more financial skill than someone who does something more balanced for a living. However, much of what I know has not been learned from books but from listening to my clients' words, by observing their behavior and life choices with regard to money—and then stopping to consider what I have seen and heard. There is deep value in a look inside oneself, self-reflection if you will, as well as a look at the facts, a simple approach that has become lost by thought-flooded, anxious Americans. Although I poke fun at our ill-fated grasps at security or riches, it is a gallows humor that I should not let mask my true concern for the personal financial challenges we all face.

At one time, I had spent a couple of years writing a draft of a book to help people invest better from their own wisdom in a world without guarantees. But the business of writing what was going to be yet another self-help financial book became tedious and removed from actually providing something of use. It isn't about the information or methodology that you can convey, it is about the method of conveyance and the audience to which you wish to communicate. You need a catchy system, the editor said, to deliver a specific number of steps, and workbook exercises at the conclusion of each chapter. You need to give readers something to do, something to fill in or complete. Oh, and a book like this today is more easily published if you have a platform. That means you need to have a website with unique users who you can count and then guarantee will buy the book. They wanted to know what "markets" I was after. Corporate executives? Financial planners and advisors? The mass affluent (moderately rich)? Or dysfunctional debtors (middle class and lower)?

Financial publishers these days want a multi-media star, someone to get on television, radio, (now it would be to tweet and to Facebook too), and to get out there on the road offering seminars, maybe work the minor leagues at an event headlined by Trump at an Expo Center. I sensed I would need whitened teeth, darkened hair, and speech coaching while subsisting on fish and weeds swallowed with spring water in airport lounges between flights and sets of abdominal work-outs. I wouldn't have had the conviction or stamina to sustain such a career leap, let alone the required regimen of tanning my skin.

Over those two years of thinking, writing, and some agonizing self-reflection, I learned that I was like the boy protagonist at the conclusion of James Joyce's great short story, "Araby," who sees himself as "a creature driven and derided by vanity." Rather than pursue a vault to my fated constellation or a flight by the sun, I came to realize that I was going to do my best for my clients and their families, the ones who had placed their trust in me, those few who seemed to appreciate what I was offering. My newsletters became my small and quiet versions of what Bruce Springsteen did with *Thunder Road*, his invitation to the world to come on a journey with him, when he began to develop his adult voice and knew that he wanted to connect with an audience about his observations, his beliefs, and his characters—his people. Like William Carlos William in Paterson, NJ, my search for meaning would have to come from the daily work of my practice, from a life lived, which would provide the kind of ongoing communication and mutual growth that I needed to sustain myself, my clients, and, hopefully, my family.

It was through my own newsletters that Al Neill, son of Humphrey B. Neill, and I became acquainted. Al showed me around his family's old Vermont farmhouse. He described his father as having had a "peppery" personality with no formal college education but an insatiable curiosity to learn. This hunger for knowledge is evinced by the various rooms in the home that were converted to studies over the years. As if the house were not large enough to contain this passion, Humphrey B. Neill ran out of space for his books after converting yet another room, an upstairs bathroom in this case, to a small library and went out to the barn to build and fill more bookcases. Throughout his writings, Neill, like a cheerful Sherpa or curious, distinctly American philosopher and teacher, provides suggested texts to his readers for further study, gestures that would be hard to envision being made by today's popular financial writers.

During the first of my stays, I occupied Humphrey B. Neill's main study, also doubling as an upstairs bedroom, the walls lined with full bookcases from floor to ceiling. There I read through Neill's own newsletters and correspondence with money managers as luminary as Ed Johnson II of Fidelity fame and fortune. Johnson personally held a subscription to Neill's *Letters of Contrary Opinion* as did several of his colleagues when the firm created one of Fidelity's flagship funds, the *Contrafund*, based on Neill's contrary approach. At that time, Fidelity as an entire firm managed about $3 billion dollars. Humphrey B. Neill apparently held the first share of *Contrafund*, a fund that in May of 2010 managed over $65 billion in assets.

Al Neill explained to me how gratified his father was to have readers far and wide, readers of the highest education who subscribed to his *Neill Letters of Contrary Opinion*. To stimulate further discussion and debate, his father held popular forums in Vermont each fall where Wall Street big-boys and individual contrary folk from various backgrounds gathered to improve their thinking on various topics of interest and concern. To this day there still exists a famous Contrarian investment conference in Vermont, a land that seems natural for the practice of going against the grain of accepted or budding conventional wisdoms.

Humphrey B. Neill's work, by its very nature, its proposed observation of crowd formation behavior and counsel to think contrarily in order to be better informed, is resistant to the type of mass popularity evident in the financial books of today. And that engrained marginality is what makes Neill's way of seeing the world and being in it so helpful today. As William Blake wrote, "Wisdom is sold in the desolate market where none come to buy." Well, some have come to buy Neill's *Art of Contrary Thinking;* it has remained in print for more than 50 years gathering significance and relevance.

The rigor and curiosity evident in Neill's writings fill the void for a reader hungry for understanding or a way to think through the dizzying 24 hour cable news cycles and the attendant, superficial sensationalism that bombard us in modern life. Think of the sound bites, more like efficient blasts utilized to impact our fears around Y2K, SARS, 9/11, the 2000 tech wreck, or the Meltdown of 2008 that oozed into March, 2009 causing pundits to predict that an appetite for stocks would never return. (The Dow then rose from about 6,500 to 11,200, a gain of more than 70% in about 13 months.) Do you remember the feel of the gathering mass opinion surrounding each of those events? Neill warns us of the inherent wrongness of crowds at extreme moments.

In addition to our fears, Neill also teaches us how to limit the damage we can do ourselves through greed and our human proclivity toward mania. Do you remember when marketers sold us the idea that oat bran was the cure-all making its way into our cereal, crackers, bread, and bagels? Where is oat bran now? Relegated to a few specialty products in the bread aisle? Think about our ongoing national obsession with low fat diets. There was a time when everyone seemed to eat bagels, which had almost no fat, while swilling diet drinks hand over fist in an effort to combat the "bulge". Soon after, Dr. Atkins taught us that those bagels were full of evil carbohydrates and showed us how to live thinly in an insulin-shocked state of starvation eating meat plates intermittently like ravenous cavemen while avoiding said carbs as if they were poisonous mushrooms. I remember the plummet of stocks related to pasta and bread. Those companies survived and thrived once more as has obesity and financial ignorance.

Neill believed that a large and quickly gathering mass of opinion provided the perfect backdrop for the most accurate counterarguments. One of the most successful money managers of our current time, Jeremy Grantham, has focused his firm's research on bubbles, how to capitalize on them when they begin to form but to be long gone when they pop. Like Neill, Grantham knows that when hot money, like hot air, comes whooshing in, there are a variety of other investments that don't receive the capital they deserve from the supposedly efficient marketplace. Today one thinks of China and gold as magnets for money, but what other long term trends and ideas lie in the shadows, underpriced, less risky, and ripe for the investor connected to the pulse of the universe but not driven mad by its pounding in his ears. Neill cautioned against our predilection for prediction and claimed that his contrarian methodology was not after accurate forecasts per se; instead, he focused on probable anticipations, which were often borne from following opposite thinking to mainstream ideas.

Can you imagine what Neill would have thought of Larry Kudlow on CNBC pushing his guests to say in one word (because the advertisements need to run) whether the market would be up or down in 6 months? Or even better, to give old Larry a number where the Dow will be at year-end?

I have marveled at Neill's prescience in writing, sixty years ago, on the possible role of space in politics and commerce in years to come—this long before missile defense systems, cell phones, and satellites. It made sense to Neill decades ago that China's socialism would move toward capitalism and that our own democratic capitalism would become more socialized. Neill also provides a step by step analysis on how governments who wish to go to war prepare their case and go about manipulating the masses into the required support. As I read his work written decades before I was alive, visions of Colin Powell, Dick Cheney, and George Bush came into my mind—apparently the most recent version of an archetypal procedure. How accurate and helpful such thinking is to our sense of understanding.

In Neill's writing, we witness a methodology for understanding through internal argument, for becoming freer and more independent thinkers, and we see the author's own example on the page, his sustained drive for accuracy and truth. We have a history of this ethic in America. Thomas Paine argued in *Common Sense* that if you wanted to learn something of value, then you had better teach yourself. In Benjamin Franklin's autobiography, we learn about the man, but we also get numerous practical tips to improve ourselves, further detailed in his *Way to Wealth*. (One might argue that F. Scott Fitzgerald's modernist reprise to Franklin's daily routine is the poignant boyhood diary of Gatsby, born James Gatz, as he develops a hollow identity and an unmoored pursuit of wealth and Daisy). New England Transcendentalists like Thoreau and Emerson (in *Self-Reliance*) embraced alternate, contrary ways of finding meaning and truth in our lives; they wrote about the importance of an introspective, personal search even as they attempted to create a national cultural identity in contrast to England's. We are, in part, a culture (admirably so) of self-help traditions,

Western pioneers, seekers of salvation through craftsmanship as opposed to an Old World indentured servitude. This creates in us a real weakness for quacks, marketers, and snake oil salesmen like those shysters in Mark Twain's *The Adventures of Huckleberry Finn*.

The popular finance books of today, and the marketing departments of their publishers exaggerate and caricature, if not manipulate, our cultural vulnerability for self improvement. In our nation of the self-made, we learn from F. Scott Fitzgerald's Gatsby about the seductive possibilities of our capitalist system as well as the dark hangover, the unmooring of the soul that occurs when forming an identity divorced from heart, meaning, and authenticity.

Thirty five years after *The Great Gatsby* was published, Walker Percy wrote *The Moviegoer* in a post-Korean War 1962. Percy was termed an American existentialist. His protagonist, Binx Bolling, a stockbroker in New Orleans, begins the novel adrift and "spinning down the coast" in his fancy convertible with various pretty secretaries who come and go. Bolling suffers from a case of what he terms "the malaise," a kind of modernist haze, born from chaos and war, the diluting effect of secularism on religion, of Americanism on tradition. Untethered and free, Binx tries to escape the malaise, in dark movie theaters in the play of light, pictures, and faint romance; he notes the rising need for Americans to validate their hometowns by seeing them appear on television. When Binx finds a woman, Kate, to care for, he realizes that sometimes we just need a good "kick in the ass," that meaning is born from the search. He believes that if you are not on a search, that you have nothing and are nowhere. Ultimately, the character finds meaning and fulfillment in finding footholds in life and "handing one another along," that is connecting to others and helping them for "good and selfish reasons."

Humphrey B. Neill writes on this side of our better nature—in the impulse of the earliest Americans like Thomas Paine and Benjamin Franklin, who wanted to help their common citizens think for themselves, the Transcendentalists like Thoreau and Emerson, and with an awareness of Modernism and Existentialism of his own lifetime. The steps, recipes, and workbooks of today's finance books would have been silly to Neill, certainly antithetical to the thinking process he believed would help people. He did not seek the status analogous to today's multi-platform, mega-marketing star, the guru, which creates in consumers a fruitless search for a priest as opposed to God or wisdom or peace.

Without false promises, Neill reveals to us that we can think and succeed ourselves, and his work reminds us that "ruminating" and cogitating on the volatility of the world can make us *feel* better through understanding the ebbs and flows of group thinking and mass psychology—while not having to react to everything and by decreasing errors we might make in investments or life through too fast conclusions. For those of us who manage money, we know how powerful it is to be wrong less often.

It is important to note that Neill refers to contrary thinking as an "art," decidedly not a science. For most of us, it's not easy to accept that thinking effectively on life, investments, and our own happiness is a work of creativity. It's hard because we are not used to it—that we need to search and to be open and perhaps to build our own lists, as opposed to following someone else's. It takes a long time to feel like we're making progress and is a continuous process of balance and footholds against a mountain of challenges. I have learned this in my own life, from my most prosperous clients, who are creative, contrary and often entrepreneurial, common people doing uncommon and personally suitable things that others would not try. Neill knew that over time and with persistence, wisdom would come, but it would come from within, not from without—in opposition to the crowd.

Humphrey B. Neill was most interested in "the human side of the market," and it is clear that he was a pioneer in the rapidly evolving behavioral finance subset of economics. We know now that people and markets are *not* rational in the here and now, and we'd better pay attention to human behavior if we want to progress in our thinking. Neill was also one of our first contrarians, a now overused and misunderstood moniker. So it is enormously helpful to return to the original source, here in Neill's work, and to understand the contrarian's simultaneous connection to the tides of humanity as well as the necessary self-protection in constructing contrary positions. His defense of individualism—our ability to develop a sense of proportion and common sense, to cultivate a rational long term view or one from high above—reminds me of yet another uniquely American moment in literature. In Ralph Ellison's *Invisible Man,* written in 1953 around the time of the first edition of Neill's *Art of Contrary Thinking,* the unnamed narrator tells us that "on the lower frequencies," he speaks for us, the readers, those who will listen. And this is where we find the simple wisdom of a self-made Vermonter who offers us a hand with our worries and concerns, who teaches us to teach ourselves, guidance for those of us who accept the invitation.

Let us occasionally put aside speculation and market worries. When we do get away from them, they become dwarfed and lose their disturbing aspect.

I am writing this in the shade of a hundred-and-twenty-five-year-old Vermont maple, and can look through its massive branches to green pastures beyond. A delightful, century-old house and neighborly barns somehow bring a quieting philosophy, and a peaceful perspective upon the problems of Wall Street. We need to get away frequently in order to realize that market fluctuations are not the all-important facts in life. If "business leaders" would desert their conferences, their gold clubs, Rotary Clubs, and merger meetings, and run away from everything, deep into the country, I am sure that they themselves would be happier, as well as make our business lives pleasanter and more evenly tempered. It does little good to leave Wall Street for summer resorts where stock tickers and business gossip continue. If you do go away, get beyond the fringe of advertising billboards and chambers of commerce. Seek the woods and hills; visit the villages where bread and butter are earned by the sweat of the brow, and where, evenings and Sundays, you join in good fellowship with your neighbors instead of in worship of the Almighty Dollar.

—from Neill's Tape Reading and Market Tactics (1931-original publication, 1959—special reprint)

THE ART OF CONTRARY THINKING

THE ART OF contrary thinking may be stated simply: Thrust your thoughts out of the rut. In a word, be a *noncomformist* when using your mind.

Sameness of thinking is a natural attribute. So you must expect to practice a little in order to get into the habit of throwing your mind into directions which are opposite to the obvious.

Obvious thinking—or thinking the same way in which everyone else is thinking—commonly leads to wrong judgments and wrong conclusions.

Let me give you an easily remembered epigram to sum up this thought:

> When everyone thinks alike, everyone is likely to be wrong.

In order to stimulate your interest in the subject of this pamphlet—namely, the art of contrary thinking—let me offer this second thought: If you wish to keep from guessing wrong, learn to think contrarily.

In the pages that follow you will find in the first section (titled "It Pays to Be Contrary") a running story of the Theory of Contrary Opinion. In the second section you will find a series of brief essays covering ideas pertinent to contrary thinking.

In presenting the subject in this manner I think you will find it broken down in such fashion that it is not only easily reviewed but also, I hope. somewhat entertaining to read.

thinking to modern interpretations. It is said, you know, that "history repeats." This is an accurate saying, but you will find that whereas history does often repeat, it never seems to repeat in exactly the same manner or in the same fashion.

One can learn a vast amount concerning the subject of mob psychology by studying past manias and past episodes, but in each case it is important to analyze the impetus which motivated the particular mania, or the fad which overtook people at a given time.

For example, one would not expect another land boom and mania in Florida with characteristics similar to the land boom which occurred in Florida in the mid-twenties.

Another example from more recent times would be the successful political campaign which former President Harry S. Truman conducted in the fall of 1948. At that particular time his tactics and his strategy—all of which, by the way, were in full accord with the principles of mob psychology—those tactics probably would not work again in just the same manner. Indeed, when he went out to support the Democratic candidate in 1952, Mr. Truman's similar strategy was unsuccessful. Many observers felt that Mr. Stevenson, for example, might have had a better chance in 1952 if Mr. Truman had not tried to repeat his tactics of 1948. I am simply passing this along as an illustration of how the appeal to the crowd may work at one time, whereas at another it will have an entirely different result.

To bring this introduction down to a conclusion, let me repeat:

The art of contrary thinking consists in training your mind to ruminate in directions opposite to general public opinions; but weigh your conclusions in the light of current events and current manifestations of human behavior.

It may appear to some readers as though the theory of contrary opinion, or the art of contrary thinking, is a cynical one. I do not think it is at all. I believe it is merely a matter of getting into the habit of looking on both sides of all questions and then determining from your two-sided thinking which is the more likely to be the correct version—which in turn leads to the correct conclusion.

Finally, let me emphasize here the factor of propaganda. We are mentally swamped today with all forms of propaganda. It pours out in millions of words. Obviously, propaganda is for the purpose of influencing minds. Therefore, it is essential to look upon both sides of public and economic questions in order to avoid being entrapped by the propagandists.

HUMPHREY B. NEILL

Saxtons River, Vermont

THE ART OF CONTRARY THINKING

BEFORE YOU BEGIN-

Here's a brief summary of the theory of contrary opinion, from which the art of contrary thinking is developed.

F OR A quick look, and to become acquainted with the theme of contrary thinking, prior to reading what follows, this brief summary is presented; it is an answer in as few words as possible to the question: "What is the Theory of Contrary opinion?"

1. Primarily, it is a method of ruminating over a broad range of public questions; political, economic, and social. The object of contrary thinking is to challenge generally accepted viewpoints on the prevailing trends in politics and socio-economics. In sum, the purpose is to contest the popular view, because popular opinions are so frequently found to be untimely, misled (by propaganda), or plainly wrong.

   a. Experience with contrary thinking warrants the use of such sloganized expressions as these:
   When everyone thinks alike, "everyone" is likely to be wrong. . . . When writers write alike, readers are prone to think alike. . . . Too many predictions spoil the forecasts; or, to put it another way, the weight of predictions causes their own downfall. (What happens is that counteracting policies are adopted to offset, or by-pass the "expectancy.")

   a. Caution: The contrary theory is a way of thinking, but let's not overweigh it. It is more of an *antidote* to general forecasting than a system for forecasting. In a word, it is a thinking tool, not a crystal ball. It forces one to think through a given subject. As has been said: If you don't think things through, you're through thinking.

2. Human traits that make the theory of contrary opinion workable, include:

Habit	Emotion	Irritability
Custom	Greed	Pride-of-Opinion
Imitation	Hope	Wishful Thinking
Contagion	Credulity	Impulsiveness
Fear	Susceptibility	Conceit

3. The theory is based upon "laws" of sociology and psychology, among which these are logically related:

   a. A "crowd" yields to instincts which an individual acting alone represses.

   b. People are gregarious; instinctively they follow the impulses of the "herd."

   b. Contagion and imitation of the *minority* (follow-theleader) make people susceptible to *suggestion*, to *commands*, to *customs*, to *emotional motivation*.

   c. A crowd never reasons, but follows its emotions; it accepts without proof what is "suggested" or "asserted."

Now, for an equally brief survey of some uses and examples of Contrary Thinking:

1. Let me start out with a socio-political thought, as it may suggest a broader application than some reference to, say, a crowd stampede in the stock market.

   a. You will agree, I think, that socialism is kin to communism.

   b. Yet, millions of people (an immense "crowd") who are socialistically inclined believe they are anticommunistic. They delude themselves. No greater (or more menacing) delusion prevails. Socialism leads to communism. To root out communism it is essential to weed out socialism. This, admittedly, is a herculean task—one unlikely to be accomplished in our lifetime.

The foregoing is an example of approaching a problem hind-end-to: the contrary approach. In all public questions which engage people's minds the contrarian tries to see in behind the surface opinions (as above, that people fail to recognize the kinship between the two isms)

2. Consider the contrary questioning of propaganda wlnich so prevalent today.

 a. It is the reasons *behind*, not the mere words *in* speeches, pronouncements, and articles which we have to seek. *Why* is the message circulated?—not simply *what* is in the message. Quite frankly, the contrarian needs to be cynical in this propaganda analysis, but so long as "opinion-makers" are out to sway and mold public opinion the only defense is "to doubt all before you believe anything"—and to look behind the words for meanings.

3. Manias and waves of mass sentiment—and crowd beliefssweep across nations when least expected. And they change just as swiftly. History is full of stories of tulip manias, South Sea bubbles, Florida land booms, and Ponzi schemes.

 a. More concretely, these examples might be mentioned, when a contrary view would have been the correct one to hold: That (in 1929) we reached a New Era and a new plateau of permanent prosperity. . . . That (in the 1930's) we had reached economic maturity. .. . That (in the 1920's) radio would put the record player and records out of business for all time. . . . That (currently) television will kill off the movies. (The contrary view here is that people are gregarious—like to go out and mingle with the crowd. Public entertainment is as old as history and it is a safe contrary opinion that human nature has not changed. Solitary entertainment will never satisfy the masses. In the long run television will enlarge the audiences, will *create* greater entertainment demands.) . We might add one more example—that of 1945, when it was widely predicted that an immediate postwar slump would find eight million out of work.

You will see, if you pursue the subject, that acquiring the art of contrary thinking is a fascinating study. The following pages leave ample scope for adding your own thoughts to those of the author's.

SECTION I

IT PAYS TO BE CONTRARY

"As a general rule, it is foolish to do just what
other people are doing, because there are almost
sure to be too many people doing the same thing."

—WILLIAM STANLEY JEVONS
(1835-1882)

IT PAYS TO BE CONTRARY

STIMULATED by the reference in *Life*,[1] there has been a growing and serious interest in the "Theory of Contrary Opinion." Considerable curiosity has been aroused concerning the art and usefulness of contrary thinking in appraising economic and sociopolitical trends.

The purpose of this section, therefore, is twofold:

1. To reply rather extensively to the numerous inquiries received that ask: "What is this Theory of Contrary Opinion?"

2. To attempt to explain the usefulness of contrary thinking asad to show that "it pays to be contrary."

You will have to forgive the author if he makes generous use of the vertical pronoun because much of what follows is personal history.

The Theory of Contrary Opinion is not something that one reads about in books or histories. There is no literature on the subject. Nothing has been written directly on the use of contrary opinions that I am aware of, except an excellent chapter pertaining to "contrary market opinions" in a book on stockmarket methods.[2] In this book the author kindly refers to my writings as being the reason for including the discussion in his book.

Thus this report on a "contrary" method of analyzing economic trends. I have written many thousands of words of contrary opinion in my former newspaper columns

---

[1]*Life*, March 21, 1949, w herein appeared comment that this writer "formulated the Theory of Contrary Opinion," following which quotations from a 1947 contrary opinion were given. See "The Strange State of the Market," by William Miller.

[2]*New Methods for Profit in the Stock Market,* by Garfield A. Drew (Boston: The Metcalf Press, 1951, and subsequent editions) . An excellen t treatise on technical methods.

("The Ruminator") and in our presently published *Neill Letters of Contrary Opinion.* Here I put my thoughts and writings together in one volume.

With this prior word let us look into the subject.

I

Goethe, the great poet-philosopher, once wrote: *"I find more and more that it is well to be on the side of the minority, since it is always the more intelligent."*

Quite frankly, the urge that first sent me on a quest that ended in the Theory of Contrary Opinion was the disappointments and disillusionment that come to everyone who seeks a method to beat the stock market."

My acquaintanceship with Wall Street dates back into the ill-fated 1920's. I soon heard about the hundred and one technical systems then in vogue for predicting the swings in stock prices. Losses in market operations quickly revealed that it isn't the system but the trader or investor himself who is at fault.

Take many chart-reading ideas, as an example. One can interpret charts almost any way he wishes. He can read into their "formations" just about any probable result he hopes for. Which is to say, that if one is bullish at heart his chart reading is likely to be interpreted optimistically; if bearishly inclined, charts accommodatingly will "say" that the market is going down. During one-way market trends (whether up or down) the trends are clearly enough defined on the charts; but when the market comes to an impasse and everybody is in a quandary as to the direction prices are likely to go, then the charts, too, are usually "silent."

On numerous occasions in the past I recall technical students of the market arguing about the probable coming trends and almost without exception each person would interpret "technical action" in accordance with his deep-seated personal opinions. In other words, the enemy of speculative success—wishful thinking—usually made the decisions.

With all respect for proponents of technical market-analysis methods, I doubt very much if any so-called "technical method" will ever completely enable people to overcome their inherent traits of hope, greed, pride-of-opinion, and similar human failings that make successful speculation one of the most difficult arts to master. (I might inject that "technical methods" refer to trend forecasts made up on the basis of the market's action in both volume and prices as well as other data.)

So it was that I soon learned (the hard way) that not only were individual opinions frequently wrong but that *my own* judgment was often unprofitably faulty.

Accordingly, I turned to a study of mass psychology in the hope of finding the answer to the riddle of "why the public is so often wrong" (and that meant why I was so often wrong). I dug into old books on the manias of speculation; I read everything I could get my hands on that pertained to the actions of crowds.

Also, my work gave me an opportunity to write on this subject of "human nature in finance" which, of course, was most instructive. There is nothing more helpful, if you wish to learn about any subject, than to write on it as well as to study it. For two or three years I wrote a little monthly house organ titled *if, As and When*,[3] containing brief essays on human foibles as they appeared in finance. The "Market Philosopher" and the "Market Cynic" were two chaps who discussed the market and economic affairs in the little magazine. Perhaps you will be amused at what my mouthpiece, The Market Cynic, wrote when things were black in late 1930:

TEN WAYS TO LOSE MONEY IN WALL STREET
by
The Market Cynic

After many hours of toil and deep thought I have compiled a dependable guide for stock traders. I shall not attempt to explain or qualify these precepts, realizing that my readers will doubtless follow them regardless of any advice to the contrary.

    1. Put your trust in board-room gossip.
    2. Believe everything you hear, especially tips.
    3. If you don't know, guess.
    4. Follow the public.
    5. Be impatient.
    6. Greedily hang on for the top eighth.
    7. Trade on thin margins.
    8. Hold to your opinion, right or wrong.
    9. Never stay out of the market.
    10. Accept small profits and large losses.

As an antidote to reckless trading or investing habits, we might insert here the admonition of Russell Sage who, when asked how he founded his fortune, replied: "By buying straw hats in January."

---

[3]This led to the authorship in 1931 of *Tape Reading and Market Tactics* (recently reprinted by Fraser Publishing Co., Wells, Vt.), which includes about as much discussion of human action as of market action.

As my interest in the *human side* of speculation developed I also found that studies of crowd behavior were singularly helpful in interpreting other, far broader, economic forces than merely fluctuations in stock prices. Not to bore you further with personal reminiscences, let me sum up my experiences:

> First, as mentioned, I learned that individual opinions (my own as well as the next man's) are of little value—because so frequently wrong.
>
> Second, that human traits (of fear, hope, greed, pride-of-opinion, wishful thinking) are so strong in the human breast that they prevent one from being *objective*. Objective analysis of economic trends is imperative, I believe, as subjective reasoning leads to *opinionated conclusions*.

Third, that if one relies stubbornly on his own opinion he is likely to "stand on his opinion," right or wrong. No trait is stronger, perhaps, than that of defending one's opinion and of being unwilling to admit error in judgment.Admittedly, it is possible to err in gauging the contrary opinion. You often will, no doubt. I found

With these basic human equations to deal with, the next problem was to find a solution.

Early in my studies and writing I had uncovered the age-old truism, mentioned above, that "the crowd is usually wrong." History is replete with examples, a few of which we shall touch upon soon.

It was through a natural evolution, therefore, that I found what I think is a usable solution:

If individual opinions are unreliable, why not go opposite to crowd opinion—that is, contrary to general opinions which are so often wrong?

And that is how the Theory of Contrary Opinion became a favorite subject to which I have since de-. voted countless hours and numberless words! That is my excuse for venturing to offer THE ART OF CONTRARY THINKING. Let me emphasize that "contrary opinions" are of great value in analyzing *economic and political trends*, not merely to catch an occasional swing in the stock market. Market trends are symptomatic of fundamental shifts in our economy and in the world economy. In this regard they are significant, of course, but the lesser ups and downs in stock prices are of negative value and are generally unpredictable

II

Admittedly, it is possible to err in gauging the contrary opinion. You often will, no9 doubt. I found in my own case that it took several years, as a matter of fact, before I was able to weigh "public opinion" with sufficient accuracy to feel reasonably confident of the contrary conclusion. It takes time to form the habit of thinking contrarily.

Moreover, even with contrary opinions as a guide we still have to fight against personal viewpoints. For example, if you feel strongly about a certain economic situation it is difficult oftentimes to submerge your feelings and coldly gauge public opinion. So, occasionally you will misjudge public opinion because of your preconceived opinions. You will jump to the conclusion that the public opinion is as you *wish* it were, and thus, unconsciously, you become a member of the "public" and in reality think as the public does.

However, after getting into the habit of "thinking opposite" you will less frequently be subject to the old traits. Finally, you may become completely objective and become the boss over those natural human failings. When that time arrives you will be amazed at how often you are *right* when (and because) others are *wrong!* A skeptical undertaking, isn't it? But it pays in the long run.

This is the only method I have uncovered in twenty years of searching that enables one to submerge the human traits that are the enemies of clear thinking. You cannot be "opposite" to the general viewpoint (which, admittedly, will appear to be the more logical) and at the same time listen to the misleading voice of "hope" and "pride-of-opinion."

Now you may be asking yourself, "How do I go about finding out what the public opinion is?"

I grant you that you will have to peruse a pile of news and comments. However, our radios, newspapers, and magazines unload such a flood of economic news and propaganda these days, it is not difficult to get a fairly accurate cross section of what people probably are thinking about and what the composite opinion is likely to be. Also—and this is important—of what some groups *want* us to accept and believe.

A 1946 act of Congress established the CEA—the president's Council of Economic Advisers. Since that time there has been a vastly greater outpouring of economic news and comments—and opinions—than before. Because the CEA viewpoints are official, they have tremendous influence upon public opinion.[4]

Official "economic releases" are especially important to analyze and weigh for their effect on the public. By the way, when we speak of "the public" it includes businessmen, too. Do not think that the public is simply the people hanging around street corners. The public is everybody, including you and me. A consensus of businessmen—or brokers— or any group—is valuable in making an analysis of opinions "to be opposite to" because of their influence on general sentiment.

Mention of the CEA brings to mind a remark made in January, 1950, by Dr. Edwin G. Nourse, former chairman of the Council of Economic Advisers. His comment was of particular interest to this writer because one always gets a kick out of seeing his pet theories confirmed by prominent speakers. Dr. Nourse was addressing a business group on the outlook for 1950 and noted that forecasters had agreed "with a unanimity that is surprising." He then added these pertinent words: "When all forecasters agree, that is the time to watch out."

To illustrate this group-opinion idea, let me give you the result of an SEC survey after the market crash of September, 1946. The Securities and Exchange Commission examined the literature sent out by 130 broker-dealers and 36 investment advisers during the week of August 26 to September 3. This was the week that preceded the precipitous

---

[4]The CEA, under President Eisenhower, may not publicly air its views as often as under President Truman, but it will be influential on opinions (especially businessmen's opinions) nevertheless. Several of the prominent business organizations are equally influential—such as the CED (Committee on Economic Development), the NAM (National Association of Manufacturers), ABA (American Bankers' Association), the United States Chamber of Commerce, and others. Likewise, tile great labor unions have powerful influence and are becoming forceful in economic education and propaganda.

drop of twentysix points in the Dow-Jones industrial average.

GENERAL M ARKET AITITUDE ON LONG-TERM OUTLOOK

Number of Letters and Wires

Bullish without qualification.................................260
Bullish, but uncertain on day to day
    market action...97
Cautious..74
Definitely bearish and/or advised selling
    at least part of holdings................................20
Inconclusive..38

_489_

In other words, only 4.1% of the professional comment and advice at this major market juncture was correctly bearMi which may be regarded as a normal expectation rather than otherwise.[5]

Group opinion naturally influences the more general or universal opinion. So, we have to look for group opinions that are found in various publications, and in the metropolitan newspapers that have large business-news sections. Numerous other publications lend side lights on what public viewpoints are—*or are likely to become.*

From a number of diversified publications you get a "feel" of prevailing general business and economic thought—and often hints of what opinions are likely to be. As the mass of people is prone to "follow the leaders," wide reading of current news and business bulletins give clues to public thought and sentiment.

---

[5]Statistics and comment taken from the chapter on the "Theory of Contrary Opinions" in Drew's book, previously mentioned.

Then, too, just talking with people gives one a slant on public thinking. You will recall how frequently in the years after World War II you heard the same reaction about business: a slump was a sure thing. Yet, each year the slump was "post- poned." A slump will set in again sometime, of course, but probably *not when universally anticipated*.

By mid-1955 the idea that "a slump is just around the corner" had swung full circle to the thought that "There'll never be another serious slump." This "new" New Era idea would also be doubted by contrarians!

A contrary opinion may call for antedating, aswell as for postdating: the point is that *general* opinions may sometimes be "late" in timing, not necessarily early.

III

Let us now review a few instances in recent history when forecasts and opinions proved wrong.

Just before World War II ended, government economists predicted a severe postwar depression (of the magnitude of 1921) . They looked for unemployment to total eight million workers. This idea took hold of the public mind, also. "Everyone" remembered (or had read about) the collapse in 1920-21, following the first World War. People jumped to the conclusion that "it would be the same this time." As we now know, it was quite different. There was no slump; the opposite occurred.

However, this idea of a postwar recession became a fixation in people's minds. During the postwar years the thought of "recession" was an obsession. The result was that business, being frightened and fearing a sudden slump, played a conservative game. At the same time, the public's appetite for goods of all descriptions was so intense that inflation set in and people spent money right and left. The result: good business, indeed a boom, instead of the much-advertised recession.

The Korean war upset all recession calculations in 1950; war-emoted people rushed to buy all manner of goods because they feared "shortages." By early 1951 speculation was rife and reckless predictions became common. Perhaps the most generally "wrong" common viewpoint was that inflation would continue

in high gear—whereas a contrary analysis took deflationary factors into consideration and the contrary view proved to be the correct one.

Incidentally, it is informative to note how a contrary opinion on inflation called the turn very accurately on government-bond prices in February, 1951 (at the time of the famous U.S. Treasury-Federal Reserve Board "accord").

It is a characteristic side light on the contrary theory that during the constantly changing phases of the economic cycle one wonders "if it will work this time." Backward glances demonstrate the theory; the future naust be checked as the months roll by.

So let us go back for a moment to the first World War. It is informative to read what a noted financial editor wrote in his descriptive memoirs. Alexander Dana Noyes had this to say of the postwar fears of late 1918:

Regarding the probable course of postwar finance and industry, complete bewilderment had captured all of us. Even during the war it had been difficult to determine whether financial markets hoped for a return to peace, or feared it. All experienced men had expressed, in private conversation, the greatest possible uneasiness as to what would happen when the war orders stopped almost overnight with our own productive industries geared-up, in prices, in working costs, in expanded plant and working personnel, to Europe's wartime purchases.

What actually occurred at first was in line with apprehensions: a swift downward plunge of prices [only minor in the stock market-H.B.N.]; 40 to 50 per cent curtailment of manufacturing production within two or three months; dismal talk of immediate hard times in business and of disfrom the mills at the moment when the thousands of laborers drafted into the army during 1917 and 1918 were returning to compete for jobs.

But almost before the community at large had adjusted its mind to that calamity, the whole picture changed so suddenly that, before we knew it, the country had rushed into a carnival of wild industrial speculation, of rising prices, of "labor scarcity" and of the highest 1,vages ever paid.

With that occurrence there began the long series of unexpected turns, of unfulfilled predictions, of complete reversal of confident expectations, which made up our financial and industrial history during the next ten years.[6]

Thus we see a similarity between the two postwar periods. The totally unexpected boom and inflation of thirty-five years ago only lasted into May, 1920, but it turned the tables on the forecasters while it lasted—and in consequence the lightninglike bust of 1921 struck with business and the public unprepared. The result was disastrous for numerous businesses; yet it paved the way for the great seven-year prosperity.

---

[6]*The Market Place—Reminiscences of a Financial Editor* (Boston: Little, Brown & Co., 1938). A "recommended" book for students of finance and contrary opinions. (Out of print, but in libraries.)

It may be seen from these references that a contrary opinion may be a valuable guide for the major economic trends.

IV

In order to note the contrast of public thought with the longer trends in the stock market it will be worth while, I think, if we review the movement of stock prices—both in the United States and in Great Britain—during the past war. There were some thoroughly interesting examples of how prices reflected future developments months ahead of what was "logically" feared or expected.

We need to get a starting point for our survey of American and British price trends, so let us go back to 1937. At the beginning of 1937 the British index of industrial shares ended its long climb from the bottom of the international depression in 1932. Coincidently, American prices also were approaching their 1937 high points.

Price trends were similar, therefore, during that recovery period.

Both in the United States and in Great Britain prices started downward in 1937. The American collapse was severe. The American market found "bottom" in March-April of 1938, but the British index continued to slide downhill until mid-1940.

On September 1, 1939, Hitler marched into Poland — but to "everyone's" surprise the New York stock market, after a brief one hour's onslaught of selling, shot upward and in the space of a few days the Dow Jones industrial average had advanced better than twenty-five points. This was a "surprise" to Wall Street and to the public because the general opinion had been that stocks would crack first and later rush up—as they did in 1914. (In 1914 the market was closed in time to prevent a panic, and when it opened some months later the big war market commenced.)

British prices, too, rallied when the actual war started in 1939, but not as sensationally as in New York..

Following this initial "war rally" both markets clung to what was called a "plateau" as the first Cold War (we might say, although it was called the "phony war" in the winter of 1940) set in in Europe. Hitler "sat out" the winter, you remember, and it was not until May 10, 1940, that he started his "blitzkrieg" across Europe. Stock prices in the meantime idled through the waiting months.

I recall especially the morning when our radios fearfully announced that the Nazis had invaded Holland and Belgium. On the commuters' train into New York that morning the conversation finally got around to the stock market. The consensus was pronounced that the market again would spurt upward —as it had in September—because the phony war was over and the real thing had commenced. I remember I was twitted about the contrary theory, as I usually brought it into the conversation when we talked about economics or the stock market. My companions, however, were thinking of the "warmarket profits" they were going to make and paid not the slightest attention to the idea of "being contrary."

The market, as it usually does, fooled everybodythis time by doing nothing!

The very quietness of the market was ominous. If prices did not rush upward as expected, then what? We did not have long to wait to find out.

On May 14, when the German armies invaded France, the flood gates opened and instead of a renewed bull market, prices crashed. In a matter of days forty-five points were shed from the industrial average.

It was a contrary development of resounding emphasis!

The British index suffered equally.

Preconceived opinions went by the board. The famed French Maginot Line was little more than an imaginary line to hold back the Germans; the Holland dikes that were to flood out any invader proved useless; the French army literally folded up.

The Western world awoke to the realization that everybody's opinion about Hitler and the Nazis was woefully wrong. An instance of a contrary opinion on an event as profound as a total war.

The June, 1940, juncture, when British and American prices both hit bottom with a thud, proves (in retrospect) to be very enlightening.

Britain, of course, was in the war and we were not. When everything looked the blackest—practically hopeless for Great Britain, as she was to be alone from then on in combating Hitler—British prices started slowly to climb upward—and never stopped their dogged advance until January, 1947!

In other words, in the face of the fall of France, tragic "Dunkerque," and the air battles over Britain, the British share market said to a frightened world that England would never go down. Share prices shared Winston Churchill's supreme faith that Hitler would never overrun Great Britain.

I think this record from war history is informative and so I have taken a good deal of space to outline it here. What of Wall Street in the meantime?

Our stock market recovered after the break of 1940, but prices started to fall off again in 1941 as if to foreshadow our entrance into the war. At the time of Pearl Harbor there was a slight rally but the market continued down until April, 1942,[7] as you doubtless remember.

Then, when the outlook appeared the blackest for us when Singapore was overrun, Bataan was lost, and Corregidor given up—the stock market stopped going down, as if to say, "Here, this hopelessness has gone far enough. From here on America is going to win the engagements." In fact, the bottom of the long decline coincided almost to the day with the fall of Corregidor. Yet, up to that moment we had been losing. Stock prices had a far keener foresight than we, the people!

Enough of recent war history to demonstrate the nutnerous times when contrary opinions were more accurate than general opinions. Let us now turn back to older history and note some principles of crowd psychology.

V

For a moment we shall drop back three centuries. In 1634 one of the most extraordinary public manias in all recorded history took place in Holland. To this day it is referred to

---

[7]This writer sent an article to the *Financial World*—it was published March 25, 1942— that was titled "Harvest Time Ahead for Contrary Thinkers." In this article contrary viewpoints were presented that "those who have the nerve to 'cross' the gloomy public, pessimistic Wall Street and bearish forecasters, will have the pleasure to turn *profitably pessimistic* when present-day bears become optimistic bulls."

as "The Tulipmania." The rage to own tulips—particularly rare specimens—engulfed the entire nation. It is impossible for us to visualize this craze, but it happened. There is no doubt about that.[8]

Prices for tulips reached fantastic heights. By 1636 the demands for tulip speculation caused rare species to be traded in on the stock exchanges of Amsterdam and other Dutch cities. Soon everybody was gambling in tulips. Like all manias, the author tells us, "everyone imagined that the passion for tulips would last forever, and the wealthy from every part of the world would send to Holland, and pay whatever prices were asked for them. The riches of Europe would [then] be concentrated on the shores of the Zuyder Zee, and poverty banished from the favoured clime of Holland."

Tulip jobbers, like stockjobbers, speculated in the rise and fall of "tulip stocks." For a while everybody made money. Many individuals grew suddenly rich, the author tells us—and "Nobles, citizens, farmers, mechanics, seamen, footmen, maid-servants, even chimney-sweeps and old-clothes-women, dabbled in tulips."

As the mania spread people did the most outrageous things to get in on the get-rich-quick tulip game. Homes and properties were sold at ridiculous prices to get cash for tulip speculation.

---

[8]You can find the whole story entertainingly described in a wonderful book entitled *Memoirs of Extraordinary Popular Delusions and the Madness of Crowds*, by Charles D. Mackay, L.L.D. First published in London, in 1852, there is now an American edition with a fore-word by Bernard M. Baruch (reprint ed.; Farrar, Straus & Cudahy, Inc., N.Y.; inquire of Fraser Publishing Co., Wells, Vt.). Mr. Baruch has remarked that he considers this book on manias essential reading for anyone who wishes to understand crowd psychology.

The mania spent itself, of course, as all such mass hysterias do, but it left in its wake countless broken pocketbooks. When the collapse came prices fell far faster than they rose. Then, as so often happens, people turned to the government for some relief from their financial distress. The whole complicated aftermath was finally referred to the Provincial Council at The Hague and it was confidently expected that the wisdom of this body would invent some measure by which credit would be restored." The mania had been so widespread that all business was affected and the general financial situation of the nation put in jeopardy. This august body, however, deliberated and stalled. They could think of no cure-all for the morning after, so they "allowed the matter to rest" and cure itself. We're told that the commerce of the country suffered a severe shock, "from which it was many years ere it recovered."

Other manias that you will wish to read about in Mackay's entertaining memoirs are John Law's "Mississippi Scheme" in France and the "South Sea Bubble" in England.° Both, strangely enough, took place at about the same time in the early 1700's. We shall not take space here to recount these speculative manias —one in paper money and the other in stocks—but they were no more fantastic than the Ponzi "borrow-from-Peter-to-pay-Paul" scheme in Boston some years ago—or, for that matter, no more ridiculous than the Florida land boom in the 1920's, when the public bought lots which were under water in back-country Florida.

---

⁹You should, I think, study John Law's monetary schemes because "Lawism" has been borrowed by modern money men.

There is no fundamental difference in the crowd psychology that becomes enmeshed in tulips from the hysteria of people today for the give-away programs on the radio.

Wherever you turn, in history or in day-to-day events, you will find that every little while a mania (differing only in degree of "madness") grasps the imagination of the "crowd" and people are carried away. We have witnessed this in any number of instances in recent years. There were "Tom Thumb golf courses," you remember, that suddenly sprouted on corner lots in every village—to last only a few months and die out. Those who "got in late" suffered losses, the same way that the public loses money in Wall Street when they attempt to play the swings of the market.

In this connection there is another book I want to call to your particular attention because it is a classic of crowd behaviorism. It was written over fifty years ago by a brilliant Frenchman by the name of Gustave Le Bon. It has been reprinted some twenty times, I believe, since it was published in the 1890's, in London. It is available in this country (The Macmillan Coinpany). The name of the book is *The Crowd; A Study of the Popular Mind*.

Le Bonn very clearly and explicitly explains the actions of crowds—what a crowd is and how a crowd reacts to various influences.

The basic distinction, of course, between a crowd and an individual is this: whereas an individual may act after reasoning and analysis, a crowd acts on feelings and emotion. Crowds follow "leaders" or follow what they assume to be the actions of leaders.

A crowd is susceptible to what Le Bon calls "contagion."

That is, if an idea attracts a few people, it is likely to spread and soon attract numbers of crowds, or tteverybody." Crowds may be made up of any number of people. Some authorities place a crowd as from five in number up; others believe a crowd consists of larger numbers. For our purpose in trying to apply contrary opinions to developments that attract public attention—or crowd attention— it makes little difference as to the number of people involved. For a trustworthy contrary opinion, the larger the public interest the better, of course.

Because a crowd does not think, but acts on impulses, public opinions are frequently wrong. By the same token, because a crowd is carried away by feeling, or sentiment, you will find the public participating enthusiastically in various manias *after* the mania has got well under momentum. This is illustrated in the stock market. The crowd—the public —will remain indifferent when prices are low and fluctuating but little. The public is attracted by activity and by the movement of prices. It is especially attracted by rising prices. Thus, in former days a "crowd" could be tempted into the market when a manipulator made a stock active and pushed its price higher.

Le Bon also tells us that a primary characteristic of a crowd is its susceptibility to "suggestion." Suggestions, in turn, are "contagious." Furthermore, Le Bon points out that "however indifferent it may be supposed to be, a crowd, as a rule, is in a state of expectant attention, which renders suggestion easy."

We can see from these definitions why it is that, say, some important announcement from official sources will have the power of "suggestibility" and shortly become contagious.

Think for a moment how common gossip will run through a town like the wind through the trees. You wonder how it is possible for a juicy bit of gossip to travel so fast! Usually, too, the stories are enlarged as they fly about. It is the same with economic and business news—or with political news.

Le Bon says, further, that a crowd thinks "in images, and the image itself immediately calls up a series of other images. . . ." When, for example, two or three years ago, there were rumors of a coffee shortage, women at once visited stores in numbers and began hoarding coffee. This was a perfect example of crowd behaviorism. They did not stop to think that the coffee would spoil if kept too long, or that probably the stories of coffee shortages were exaggerated. Crowds do not stop to think, as we have noted. The power of suggestion is what motivates their action.

From the political standpoint, it is interesting to note what Le Bon has to say about leaders' influencing crowds. It would appear that Mr. Truman had a copy of *The Crowd* in his hip pocket as he toured the nation in 1948. Listen to this, by Le Bon:

> Given to exaggeration in its feeling, a crowd is only impressed by excessive sentiments. An orator wishing to move a crowdmust make an abusive use of violent affirmations. [The no-good Eightieth Congress—at every whistle stop.] To exaggerate, to affirm, to resort to repetitions, and never to attempt to prove anything by reasoning are methods of argument well known to speakers at public meetings.

The more you get into this fascinating subject of crowd psychology the more you will agree, I think, that the human factor is a potent force in our socalled business cycle. Monetary factors are powerful, production is a basic support, yet what "people" decide to do must always receive earnest consideration.

A well-known economist for a prominent foundation devoted to economic research wrote me as follows, and I value his comment highly:

> I have believed for a long time that there was no sound and valid way to predict either major turns in the business situation or larger or intermediate turns in security prices, but of all the imperfect methods, yours offers the greatest promise [referring to contrary-opinion analysis].

In other words, some guide other than statistical evidence appears to be required if we are ever to forecast economic trends with reasonable accuracy.

Le Bon wrote a number of other books of equal significance. Most of them are difficult to obtain, except in large libraries. One—*The Psychology of Socialism*—is an eye opener to study today. It, too, was written over fifty years ago (1899). I want to take space just to give you his definition of Socialism, because it teaches us how the "isms" attract and hold extraordinary followin.gs:

> Socialism is becoming a belief of a religious character rather than a doctrine. Now the great power of beliefs, when they tend to assume this religious form . . . lies in the fact that their propagation is independent of the proportion of truth or error that they may contain, for as soon as belief has gained a lodging in the minds of men its absurdity no longer appears. . . . [Note how this latter describes the habit of people who "rationalize" events.]
>
> To the crowd, no longer satisfied with political and civic equality, it [Socialism] proposes equality of condition, without dreaming that social

inequalites are born of those natural inequalities that man has always been powerless to change.

One can think of several "movements" that have become of "a religious character" in recent years. Indeed, the social revolution in our own midst, since the inception of the New Deal, follows the Le Bon tenets.

VI

One more story from the past may serve to bring Out the subject of crowd psychology in bold relief.

Inflation reflects crowd behaviorism in all its forms of greed, fear, and cupidity. History is replete with inflation manias. In the 1920's the German and French inflations were charaeteristic—as was the Chinese inflation of the 1940's (and our own, but to a lesser degree because, fortunately, it did not "run away").

There is one historic inflation with which everyone should be familiar. Doubtless you know the story of the fiat-money inflation in France in the eighteenth century. Let us review it briefly, because the causes of the inflation and the "controls" that were attempted have a serious lesson for the world today. Time after time through history we find that when nations encounter financial difficulties the popular solution is always, "What we need is more money."

"Early in the year 1789," writes Andrew D. White in his classic monograph,[10] "the French nation found itself in

---

[10] *Fiat Money Inflation in France,* available in digest form from the Foundation for Economic Education, Irvington-on-Hudson, N.Y. A complete reprint edition is sold by The Caxton Printers, Ltd., Caldwell, Idaho.

deep financial embarrassment: there was a heavy debt and a serious deficit.

"Statesmanlike measures, careful watching and wise management would, doubtless, have ere long led to a return of confidence ... but these involved patience and self-denial, and, thus far in human history, these are the rarest products of political wisdom. . . ."

We seemingly can take Mr. White's remarks to heart as they appear to apply also to the mid-twentieth cen tur y.

In France the hard way had no appeal. There was a general search for some short road to prosperity, White tells us, and "ere long the idea was set afloat that the great want of the country was for more of the circulating medium [today, throughout the world, it is for more *dollars*] and this was followed by calls for an issue of paper."

The great Mirabeau, you remember, tried by the strength of his oratory to stop the fiendish schemes of Marat, who wished to issue paper money backed by the lands of the Church. Mirabeau lifted his voice in the National Assembly against the wicked idea of issuing four hundred million assignats unsupported by specie—but to no avail.

The immediate result of the paper-money stimulant was, of course, successful. For a brief time, business picked up and people were happy. France rejoiced at the brilliant plan.

Bootstrap economics never works for long, however. Within a short five months the money was gone and "the government was in distress again." You know the sequel. After lengthy debates wise counsel went for naught. On the twenty-ninth of September, 1790, the Assembly voted by a large majority to issue more assignats—this time doubling the amount to eight hundred million.

The false illusion that inflation is prosperity swept through France.

There was no stopping the orgy. Issue followed issue as the paper money quickly lost its value.

Soon, drastic laws were instituted to save the day. Landed estates were confiscated. Price control was tried—the "Law of the Maximum."

"New issues only increased the evil," White explains . . . "but no relief resulted save a monetary stimulus, which aggravated the disease.

"At last carne the collapse and a return, by a fearful shock, to a state of things which presented something like certainty of remuneration to capital and labor. Then, and not till then, came a new era of prosperity."

When governments, including our own, carry great debt loads, it behooves thoughtful citizens to recall occasionally the disastrous inflations of the past, the illusions of bootstrap economics—which always are accompanied by crowd hysteria.[11]

---

[11]A book that is most helpful as an aid in the recognition of "illusions"is *Popular Financial Delusions,* by Robert L. Smitley. I am happy to say that this splendid book has been reprinted by my colleague, James L. Fraser, Fraser Publishing Co., Wells, Vermont. Mr. Srnitley, now retired, is the unquestioned authority in this country on economic literature. At one time (1907-10), a member of the New York Stock Exchange, he found that his interests lay in the intellectual pursuit of books on finance rather than in the pursuit of orders on the floor of the Exchange (although he has always been an adept speculator and investor). His book business became world-wide in scope. Many a college and private library had its socioeconomic books selected by bookman Smitley. I owe R.L.S. more than I can repay for his guidance and counsel through the years and for the reading and studies he advised. I am pleased, therefore, to have this opportunity of expressing my indebtedness to him.

VII

The problem of "money" is far too complex for us to examine in this report. It is a study in itself and one which still confuses the great rninds of the world. It would be presumptuous for me to attempt a learned discussion of monetary economics.

However, I do wish to leave with you the thought that, because monetary problems *are not* comprehended by the public or by the average businessman, "money management" will continually cross up public opinions concerning economic trends.

Monetary manipulation is a crafty and tricky tool within a system of bootstrap economics. If you make it a point to become posted on some of the more common practices of monetary management you will occasionally be able to discern trends that are opposite to those commonly discussed in public pronouncements and business stories. There is no doubt that shifts in monetary policies in 1949, for example, influenced the early ending of the mild down turn in business activity. It was this marked change in policy which supported this writer's contrary opinion expressed during the first half of 1949 that the slump would again be postponed.

Just as a reminder let us record the clear-cut policy announced by the Federal Reserve Board in June, 1949: "It will be the policy of the Committee [Open Market Committee] to direct purchases, sales, and exchanges of Government securities by the Federal Reserve Banks *with primary regard to the general business and credit situation.*" [Emphasis added by this writer.]

This illustrates the part the Federal Reserve banks will play in coming tussles with the economic cycle. Former Treasury Secretary Snyder stated (1950) that debt-management policies are the responsibility "of the Secretary of the Treasury and cannot be delegated." As the Treasury demanded easy money—low interest rates—and the Federal Reserve Board intended to control money rates, we witnessed some "interesting disagreements" in the months following. (You remember -what happened: Money rates stiffened, and government bonds fell in price, following the Federal Reserve Board's later policy of withdrawing its supports from the bond market. In 1953 interest rates hardened still further and a long-term bond carried an interest rate well above 3 per cent.)

During 1955 the tussle between credit expansion and monetary restraint made news. The Federal Reserve Board was determined to curb the overextension of consumer borrowing.

The public and businessmen as a whole do not pay attention to, or comprehend, monetary strategy. It behooves contrary thinkers to bone up on the rudiments of the money market and the government bond market in order to try to measure the influences that our banking and governmental authorities may have on economic trends.

Since the world (and the United States) "went off gold," the money supply has been regulated by men in place of the metal. Money supply, therefore, has become a master key of economic forecasting.

A contrary opinion expressed by this writer early in 1951—in connection with the money problem—

was that interest rates would be forced higher and that government bonds would fall in price because of the necessity for anti-inflationary Federal Reserve policies. This is an interesting example of thinking contrarily to government propaganda. (The President and the Secretary of the Treasury meanwhile continued to beat the drums for the long-term 21/2 per cent interest rate, but the rates went up.)

The Eisenhower administration has striven for a sound-money program but towering government and "space-age" expenses have defied their full efforts.

VIII

Is the public *always* wrong?

This is probably the most frequently asked question about the Theory of Contrary Opinion. For a correct answer we need to change the words in the question.

Let me put it this way: Is the public wrong a*ll the time?*

The answer is, decidedly, "No." The public is perhaps right more of the time than not. In stockmarket parlance, the public is right *during* the trends but wrong at both ends!

One can assert that the public is usually wrong at junctures of events and at terminals of trends.

So, to be cynical, you might say, "Yes, the public is always wrong when *it pays to be right*—but is far from wrong in the meantime."

I am often asked: "How about 1928 and 1929? Wasn't the public right in the market, and wouldn't a contrary opinion have been wrong?"

The public was right in 1928, if by right you mean it was right to ride a wild whirlwind of speculation—but dead wrong in the sense that it was a foregone conclusion the public would be wrong when the final blow struck. By the same token, a contrary opinion would have been wrong in the sense that it would have been many months *previous*. In great mass speculative periods, such as 1928 and 1929, the Theory of Contrary Opinion would be *right* in keeping people out of the storm, but decidedly wrong from a measurement of interim paper profits.

Many very smart people deserted the stock market in 1928, realizing it was running far out of boundsyet many were dragged back in again by the magnetism of the gushing prices that kept on rushing up. "Everyone" was so engrossed with the rising prices that few if any gave heed to Secretary Mellon's cryptic remark in July, 1929, that "now is a good time to buy bonds." Indeed, few people had any idea what he meant—or cared!

It is to be noted that the use of contrary opinions will frequently result in one's being rather too far ahead of events. A contrary opinion will seldom "time" one's conclusions accurately.

The "time element" is the most elusive factor in economics. We need to get that fixed firmly in our minds. (Insofar as I am aware, there is *no* known method of *timing* events or trends.)

Therefore, when we adopt a contrary opinion, as a guide, we must recognize that we may be *too far* ahead of the crowd. This is because economic trends often are very slow in turning, or reversing. Frequently, opinions on a given situation will be so onesided that a contrary opinion is obvious. However, it may be some weeks, or months, before the trend of the situation alters sufficiently to make the contrary conclusion the correct one.

It is probably safe to say, however, that it is wiser to be early than to be late—in most economic decisions. This does not apply only to the stock market. Not by any ineans. It applies as well to business policies and to other economic problems.

In sum, the public is not wrong all the time—and a contrary opinion is usually ahead of time.

IX

In concluding this brief report on the Theory of Contrary Opinion we should tackle one more question: Is it difficult to *use* the contrary theory?

A hard question, obviously, because the theory is intangible. Enough illustrations have been submitted, I think, to demonstrate that if one can get into the habit of thinking "opposite" to the crowd he will be right in his thinking more often than wrong.

Admittedly, the theory is perplexing and often perverse. In the first place, it is contrary to one's natural reactions to be contrary to general opinions! Moreover, others with whom you discuss your contrary opinions will almost always violently disagree —will find numberless reasons and argutnents to show you you're wrong in your adverse viewpoints. It will be difficult to stick to your contrary viewpoints because it will seem so obvious that you should be thinking as others are. Furthermore, it often takes a long time to prove out your point. This weakens your faith, because you begin to fear your contrary ideas are the wrong ones!

To be contrary means you have to be opposed to the obvious—and that is frequently quite baffling.

Perhaps it will help this confused explanation if we listen to Sir Francis Bacon who, nearly three hundred years ago, admonished his students to "Doubt all before you believe anything! Watch your idols!"

In *Novum Organum*, this keen thinker and iconoclast established first his doubt of all things, before proceeding to his consideration of knowledge: "In general, let every student . . . take this as a rule—that whatever his mind seizes and dwells upon with peculiar satisfaction, is to be held in suspicion; and that so much the more care is to be taken, in dealing with such questions, to keep the understanding even and clear...."

This much may be said—and demonstrated conclusively, I believe—that if we *fail* to take crowd opinions into consideration, when arriving at conclusions concerning economic and political events, we shall most certainly make many errors in forecasting. Contrary thinking unquestionably helps one to avoid many common errors in forecasting—errors arising from miscalculating what the public will do.

I believe this is more likely to be the case under a managed economy than under a so-called laissezfaire system of society. For this reason: As mentioned earlier, under a managed system of society, into which we are steadily becoming more deeply in- volved, propaganda becomes an ever-more-powerful tool of the "managers."

Our minds are bombarded continually with ideas and thoughts that are planted with the avowed purpose of influencing us. We have little conception of the amount of "news" that is actually manufactured.

How to separate propaganda from actual news takes a keen mind familiar with news-gathering and propaganda agencies.

But it does not take a keen mind to estimate public opinions—and business opinions and then to sit down and analyze opposing viewpoints. It takes prac tice but it is not nearly as difficult as it may appear.

Indeed, I'll end this exposition by saying that it is far easier to be contrary to general opinions than it is to create original thought.

It *Pays* to be contrary as it may keep you from guessing wrong!

SECTION II

ESSAYS PERTAINING TO
THE THEORY OF CONTRARY OPINION
and
THE ART OF CONTRARY THINKING

"Follow the course opposite to custom and
you will almost always do well."
—JEAN JACQUES ROUSSEAU
(1712-1778)

WAVES OF MASS SENTIMENT

IN THIS first of a number of brief essays on the theory of contrary opinion and crowd psychology, suppose we take a look at the waves of mass sentiment as they are whipped up by war.

Emotions rise and fall with events—but in an ascending motion, like an incoming tide that works higher and higher. Wars stimulate feelings and actions to an abnormal pitch. Contagion (to use Le Bon's term) spreads. Patriotic fervor, growing alarm, and the instinctive hate of the enemy—all combine to arouse people to herd together for collective security. 'Wilfred Trotter" states that "the cardinal mental characteristics of the gregarious animal is his sensitiveness to his fellow-member of the herd . . . a threat against the whole herd is the intensest stimulus . . . the individual reacts toward it in the most vigorous manner. . . ." Everett Dean Martin" tells us that "every interest—excepting profit-seeking—is subordinated to the one passion to crush the enemy."

In pondering over the tides of war emotions, we may recall the warning of Arnold Toynbee that the wars of 1914-18 and 1939-45 were not "isolated or unprecedented calamities. They were two wars in a series." Moreover, the series is a "progression"—and Toynbee concludes that the last war "was not the climax of this crescendo movement."

---

[12]*Instincts of the Herd in Peace and War* (London: T. Fisher Unwin, Ltd., 1916). Timely to read and study now as in 1916-18. There is a revised edition, edited by R. W. Chapman (New York: Oxford University Press, 1953, but out of print also).

[13]*The Behavior of Crowds* (New York: Harper 8c Brothers, 1920).

However, it is important to note that the herd instinct is not fully aroused until the danger of destruction of "the whole herd" is threatened. Until the intervention of Red China in the Korean war, for example, and the probability of the war's spreading became a public fear, the six-thousand-milesaway war in Korea did not stir up people acutely.

Trotter mentioned this characteristic of crowd psychology in wartime by referring to the Boer War of 1899-1901. "This was not and was not regarded as capable of becoming a direct threat to the nation [Great Britain]." The Spanish-American War in our own history is a similar example. During the brief "phony war" in the winter of 1940 people here and abroad were indifferent to Hitler's threats.

Because of the manner in which the war in Korea expanded—plus the stupendous war program instituted in this country and the sweeping propaganda—the wave of mass sentiment commenced to roll over us early in 1951, quite in accordance with the history of wartime emotions.

However—and here is the nub—a prolonged or intense war sentiment is unlikely if a war program continues to be chiefly for *defense against war*. Thus, the waves of mass sentiment seemingly are influenced by alternatives such as these:

1. If actual warfare does not occur in a matter of months, the waves of war sentiment tend to fade out.

2. If a world-wide explosion occurs, it will prove far more calamitous than now envisaged. ("An electronic horror.")

3. If the threat of war suddenly diminishes, a public reaction against the war program and its restrictions is equally swift.

THE INVESTORS' DILEMMA

The Neill Theory of Contrary Opinion was injected not long ago into a most interesting controversy on stock-market forecasting and investment practice.

Mr. A. Wilfred May, executive editor of the *Commercial and Financial Chronicle,* stirred up the investment pundits during a speech in Chicago on December 27, 1950. He blasted the popularity of market-swing forecasting and punched out a strong case for the "value concept"—which, in brief, argues for buying *values and prospects*—as you would buy a farm or a business—instead of flirting with market swings (a policy with which this writer earnestly agrees from a retrospect of twenty-five years).

I was tossed into the discussion that followed (in "Letters to the Editor"). Mr. B. K. Thurlow, of Winslow, Cohil & Stetson, Inc., members of the New York Stock Exchange, while agreeing with Mr. May's buying policy, inquired what policies Mr. May advocated in selling. Among Mr. Thurlow's queries was this one: "Do you consider that such general psychological approaches as Neill's Theory of Contrary Opinion have their place in the strategy? . . ."

This offers an excuse to blow our contrary horn, and to mention an off-beat note.

Let us stress one psychological factor—a basic truism—that underlies the whole problem, because in the final analysis investment is a human problem.

The average investor does not think and does not wish to think. Automatic forecasting methods relieve investors from sweating it out for themselves.

They can , `read" the findings of a given market-swing method and thereby avoid the backbreaking pick-and-shovel work that is necessary if one wishes to uncover the rich pay dirt that lies deeply buried. Prospecting for true values is hard work! Mr. May's "buyvalues" concept is without question a sound approach, but it requires applied head work and mental discipline. It will never be practiced by a large segment of the public.

Thus, I dare to predict that contrary opinions will remain valid as a guide until public psychology changes—and it has not changed in centuries. So long as the investing public (and many of its advisers) acts as a "crowd," it'll pay to be contrary.

Now for an off-beat note: If one relies on the Theory of Contrary Opinion for accurate *timing* of his decisions he frequently will be disappointed.

However, this does not invalidate the theory's usefulness. There is no known method of timing economic trends—but it is known that the crowd is always wrong at IMPORTANT reversal areas in market trends. Your watch is still useful, although it may run fast; you allow for the error and recognize that you may be early for appointments, but you do not miss the train.

Further, if you adopt Mr. May's sound concept, you will have all the more reason to be contrary. A probing mind is a contrary mind. Values are seldom unearthed except by looking in the less likely spots for the unexploited medium. Contrarywise, the overvalued medium is easily overlooked when markets are ebullient and "everyone" is buying. Obviously, there are fewer "values" when the market is "high" —yet there always are some for the deep diggers, as Mr. May points out. (One might mention in order to cite an example, the gold stocks in 1929-30. . . . To echo Mr. May, it is happily my lot to discuss these academic questions as I have no investment-advisory clientele.)

HABIT

The word "habit" will appear frequently in these essays on the art of contrary thinking, so we might introduce the subject.

Habit, of course, is one of the chief studies in psychology. Habits are of various types: fixed and changeable; likewise, physical, mental, and emotional. 'William Henry Mikesell[14] tells us that "every division of the mind is habitualized." And further, that

> Everyone has thought-habits as well as habits of skill. One person can predict the general kind of judgment another person will pass ten years from now, because ways of thinking become stereotyped. Everyone has feelings-habits. Very few feelings are new and fresh; we have experienced most of them before. Attitudes are mostly feelings-habits. . . . Everyone has emotional habits and habits of perception. . . .

Through habits we develop routines of action and thinking. This applies to business and financial thinking just as it does to the daily routines of eating and dressing. As we progress up the ladder many habits of judgment become fixed. When out-of-the-ordinary problems confront us we

---

[14]Menial Ilygiene (New York: Prentice-Hall Inc., 1939).

turn from "habitual decisions," but the daily decisions in business are largely habit.

Economic and market opinions also become habitual, unless we continually refresh our minds with new ideas and historical background.

One acquires mental and physical habits early in life. More often than not these habits become fixed. As they say here in Vermont, a person is "sot in his ways."

> By way of illustration, compare in your mind the thought-habits of those who were educated and started out in business during the 1930's with those who matured in the 1920's or earlier. Countless young people were influenced by the depressed times and the advent of New Dealism in the 1930's. The result has been that it is difficult to find a common meeting ground between those with the habit of depressed thinking and those who grew up in an era of prosperity and individualism.

William James, in his noted essay on *Habit*,[15] stresses "the universally admitted fact that any sequence of mental action which has been frequently repeated tends to perpetuate itself; so that we find ourselves automatically prompted to *think, feel,* or *do* what we have been accustomed to think, feel, or do, under like circumstances, without any consciously formed *purpose,* of anticipation of results. . . . The strength of early association is a fact so universally recognized that the expression of it has become proverbial. . . ."

---

[15]New York: Henry Holt and Company, 1914. (Originally published in *Popular Science Monthly,* February, 1887; then in 1890, in James's *The Principles of Psychology.*)

Habits push our minds into ruts—and it takes a considerable amount of force and time to get out of the ruts. So, in contemplating crowd action (to which we may wish to be contrary) we have to consider not only the thought-habits of the crowd but our own thought-habits! This "rut-thinking" is regularly reflected in economics, in polities, and in the stock market.

THE PSYCHOLOGY OF INFLATION

In a little book by the late Frank Parker Stock- bridge (long out of print) , the author refers to the "first" inflation he encountered in his research as having been recorded twenty-five centuries ago. Countless inflations have occurred since. It would be amusing, if results had not usually been tragic, to note that each time the government or the dictator (and there have been more dictators than free governments in history, as you doubtless are aware) attacked the inflation from the manipulative or easymoney angle rather than from the sound course of curing the cause.

In the first inflation, Solon, who assumed supreme powers in Athens in 594 B.C., "promulgated a plan for the relief' of debtors and and the redistribution of national wealth which set the pattern other governments have followed, more or less closely for over 2,500 years."

As Mr. Stockbridge further wrote, the Greeks had a name for the cure of inflation. Solon called his plan "Seisachtheia," literally, "shaking off of burdens," which sounds curiously like some much more recent political slogans. And the means he adopted for putting Seisachtheia into effect have likewise a familiar sound. He reduced the value of the currency and cancelled agrarian debts.

Tracing various inflations down through history it is interesting to note how the "time elements" have varied. That is, how inflations have differed because of the time it has taken for the inflation to take hold —to catch fire.

It seems evident that the psychology of inflation is fully as important to study as the economic factors.

In the early 1930's when former President Roosevelt took us off the free gold standard and commenced to experiment with a different price for gold each morning, printing presses commenced to hum with books and pamphlets pertaining to inflation. Any modern bibliography on inflation contains numerous articles and pamphlets dated in the 1930's. We were all warned time and again that inflation would soon overtake us and ruin us. Yet a contrary psychology prevailed.

The public went serenely on its way, paying little heed to the dreaded fears and maintaining confidence in the dollar. The fact the dollar had been clipped in gold value meant nothing to the average person. The paper dollar in his pocket was still good. That was all he cared about. Result: no ruinous inflation. Indeed, dollars remained dormant. Turnover of money remained quiet. Inflation did not "take."

A decade and a half later signs of uneasiness and "doubt of the dollar" developed in the public mind. At the same time, the source of the inflation—monetary policy—was grudgingly being attacked. In consequence, the race between economic forces and psychology was on. A contrary view at the time (March, 1951) suggested economics would win and a runaway inflation again would be averted.

This is still a big issue before the country, because the control of inflation rests upon future monetary policies, and upon the government's management of the budget.

WHEN THERE IS NO PUBLIC OPINION

When everyone ignores a vital subject, it is likely to be important to everybody.

In employing the theory of contrary opinion you will find it necessary at times to consider subjects and economic factors concerning which the public holds no opinion and in which people generally have scant interest.

This sounds odd, perhaps, because how can one "go opposite" to no opinions?

The point is this: We are trying, in the use of contrary opinions, to calculate *trends*, and not merely indulging in academic appraisals of opinions. Thus, if certain economic factors influence trends and yet do not have public interest, we still need to consider them—because the public *will react* to the *results*.

The subjects with the greatest influence, but holding the smallest public interest, are money and banking. (Money, of course, includes "credit.")

There have been fifty-foot shelves of books wi it ten on money, credit, and banking, yet it remains a complex and little understood subject. From Ricardo to KeYnes, from John Law to Irving Fisher and Sumner Slichter, from the coin clippers of old to the moneyrate peggers of the recent past, the money jugglers have continued to toss their theories into the air.

Those of us not schooled in the intricacies of monetary economics have to be guided by simple rulesrules that we can understand, although they are shouldered aside by the pundits because they are not profound. Take for example this one:

> To limit the supply, make money scarce and dear;
> To increase the supply, make money plentiful and
> cheap.

Or this:

> Cheap money makes things dear. Inflation.
> Dear money makes goods cheap. Deflation.

True, we have to weigh conclusions with the factors of production, velocity of money-in-use, employment (purchasing power), and such items, but basically money is the root of the price level.

Caught as we are in the fog of "monetary mists," we should lower our gaze and keep our eye on the white line in the middle of the highway. We may miss the fuzzy suppositions but we shall not completely lose all sense of direction.

In times of a money crisis contrary ruminating will hold us to simple facts and to cynical queries. What are the opinions of the money managers and money jugglers? What motives have they for their actions? What axes have they to grind? Is the action contemplated experimental (like hiking the price of gold each morning) , or is it fortified with historical reasoning? Have the money managers taken the short or the long view?

Finally—based upon the past, shall we be contrary to, or in accord with, the money program as set forth? What will be the public's reaction later?

IMITATION OF THE MINORITY

A common fallacy is the idea that the majority sets the pattern and the trends of social, economic, and religious life. History reveals quite the opposite: the majority copies, or imitates, the minority and this establishes the long-run developments and socioeconomic evolutions.

If you can locate Gabriel Tarde's searching and fascinating book, *The Laws of Imitation*, get hold of it by all means. You will discover a whole new field for ruminating over the theory of contrary opinion.[16]

In an introduction by Franklin H. Giddings, then professor of sociology at Columbia, we arc introduced to Tarde in this fashion:

Among the phenomena that early arrested his ITarde's1 attention was imitation. From his office as magistrate he obse, ved the large part that imitation plays in criminal conduct. Very rapidly M. Tarde's ardent mind ranged over the field of history-, followed the spread of Western civilization, and reviewed the development of language, the evolution of art, of law, and of institutions. The evidence was overwhelming that in all the affairs of men, whether of good or of evil report, imitation is an ever-present factor; and to a philosophical mind the implication was obvious, that there must be psychological or sociological laws of imitation, worthy of most thorough study.

---

[16]Translated from the French in 1903 and published by Henry Holt & Company in the same year. Rather scarce.

Everyone has witnessed imitation in countless forms. Hollywood has been aped and imitated ever since the movies came into prominence. Prior to the advent of the socializing New Deal youngsters were taught from the cradle that they, too, might rise to be President. Horatio Alger, Jr., wrote many books that oldsters were brought up on which showed that the bootblack and the newsboy should aspire to a "brown-stone front." Imitation in the stock market is common, as the crowd follows the leaders.

Tarde's attempt at prediction, too, was notable, when he remarked that "it is safe to predict that a century of adjustment will follow upon the past century [the nineteenth] of discovery."

Invention and imitation, Tarde tells us, are elementary social acts. These, in turn, are motivated by *belief and desire*. Thus, when "invention and then imitation takes possession of belief and desire in order to organize them" they become powerful social and economic forces.

Space will not permit more than a taste to whet your appetite, but let us add these further sentences to tempt you to look up Tarde:

"... it is nevertheless true that ... belief and desire bear a unique character that is well adapted to distinguish them from simple sensation. This character consists in the fact that the contagion of mutual examples re-enforces beliefs and desires that are alike, among all those individuals who experience them at the same time. ... We no longer have epidemics of penitence ... but we do have epidemics of luxury, of gambling, of lotteries, of stock-speculation, of gigantic railroad undertakings, as well as epidemics of Hegelianism, Darwinism, etc." [to which today he would doubtless add Communism and Socialism].

FOR YOUR NOTEBOOK

A penetrating book was written about fifty years ago by Theodore E. Burton (later a United States Senator of note).[17] Unfortunately, it is out of print and difficult to locate in secondhand book departments. It should be reprinted. It was published in 1902, with later editions brought out in succeeding years. If you happen across it by all means add it to your library.

There are many contrary thoughts brought out by the author and in various quotations. Perhaps you will like to make note of two or three.

For example, in the Introduction the author refers to a comment of M. Clement Juglar, former eminent French financial writer who, in *Des Crises Commerciales* (1889) , said this: "Paradoxical as it may seem, the riches of nations can be measured by the violence of the crises which they experience."

This is thought-provoking when you consider the false delusions countless people entertain that the capitalistic system in America will break down under the onslaught of depressions. Senator Burton comments that "those countries which seem to suffer the most from these (economic) disturbances (of boom and bust) show from decade to decade the greatest increase in wealth and material prosperity."

One of our favorite quotations also appears in this book: "In making investments it is foolish to do just what other people are doing, because there are almost sure to be too many people doing the same thing." This was written by

---

[17]Financial Crises and Periods of Industrial and Commercial DePressions (New York: D. Appleton and Company, copyright, 1902).

Professor William Stanley Jevons, in his Primer of Political Economy, some seventy-five years ago. (The contrary-opinion idea is not new!)

This writer has harped (in his writings) upon the "capital waste" that results from armament production. Burton has this to say about it:

> It is also true that the destruction of wealth, as by the waste of war or improvident enterprise, and the derangement caused by the locking up of capital in preparation for future consumption, do not show their results in crisis or depression until some time has elapsed. . . . After the exhaustion of war there is, for a time, great activity in providing supplies, which have been rendered scarce by extraordinary demands. As a result, during war or a period of unusual enterprise, and for a time thereafter, the true situation is obscured by exceptional activity, by the fact that labour is generally employed, prices are high and rising, and speculation is rife. . . . ['This precisely portrays the post-World War II era; yet we were told erroneously of our prospects for an immediate slump.]

In these times, when so much is written about the "money supply" and when some observers assert that an abundance of money will forestall a slump, it is interesting to note this comment by Senator Burton: ". . . paradoxical as it may seem, the starting point for crises and depressions may be found in abundance rather than in scarcity, whether of money or capital."

ON BEING CONTRARY TO THE GREGARIOUS OPINION

Let us quickly define that harsh word, "gregarious." It means "associating together in herds"—from the Latin word for "flock."

One of the books found helpful in a study of the art of contrary thinking is *Instincts of the Herd in Peace and War,* by William Trotter, previously mentioned. The author bases his sociological thesis on "gregarious man," or the herd instincts in us humans. He asserts that "man is a gregarious animal in literal fact, that he is as essentially gregarious as the bee and the ant, the sheep, the ox, and the horse . . . and that his (man's) conduct furnishes incontestable proof of this thesis, which is thus an indispensable clue to any inquiry into the intricate problems of human society. ..."

Very briefly, with the risk of lifting thoughts out of context, let us extract Trotter's summary of the more obvious gregarious characteristics we display:

1. Man is intolerant and fearful of solitude—physical or mental. [I think we all recognize this general characteristic. The vast majority of people dislike to be alone. If we have to spend a day all by ourselves, most of us become bored with our own company within the first hour.]

2. He is more sensitive to the voice of the herd than to any other influence. [This, of course, is the theory of "following the crowd."]

3. He is subject to passions of the pack in his mob violence and the passions of the herd in panics. [Economic panics reflect this characteristic also.]

4. He is remarkably susceptible to leadership. [One immediately thinks of Hitler or Napoleon, but history books contain countless stories of mob leadership.]

5. His relations with his fellows are dependent upon the recognition of him as a member of the herd. [Here we get into the psychological excuses for "popularity contests," and into the field of modern personnel work and into the new science of "human relations in industry."]

If the habit of contrary thinking does no more than to teach us to develop our own resources—*and to like to be alone occasionally*—it would be worth while; because when alone we might fall into the habit of actually thinking through a given subject, instead of taking the other fellow's word for it. (As one writer has said: If you cannot think through a subject you're through thinking.) If we can learn to think we shall indeed be a member of the minority! An aid to thinking is found by taking prominent assertions and allowing your mind to roam over all the "opposites" and "alternates" you can think of. I call this ruminating (or chewing the cud) .

THE THEORY OF CONTRARY OPINION IS A "WAY OF THINKING"

BUT LET'S NOT OVERWEIGH IT!

This question bobs up constantly: What is this theory of contrary opinion?

The reply may be stated in a word: It is a "way" of thinking, But, let me add, let's not overweigh it! Let us give it its proper weight. It certainly is not a system to beat the horse races, or the stock market. Nor is it a crystal ball. It is plainly nothing more than developing the habit of doing what every textbook on learning advises, namely, to look at both sides of all questions. Or, as Sir Francis Bacon put it: "Doubt all before you believe. . . ."

Inasmuch as very, very few people ever take the trouble to look at both sides of questions—indeed, ever take the trouble to think very much even on one side—it is obviously of great advantage to be among the tiny minority that does exercise its brain occasionally. This is not written in an effort to be funny. It is an actual fact that the majority of people acquire information and form opinions second-hand - -from something they read hurriedly or hear with half an ear.

Let me quote a truly educated man in this connection. Albert Jay Nock, in *Memoirs of a Superfluous Man*,[18] has a number of unkind things to say about universal education, although he blames what he thinks is the failure of educa-tion more upon us, the students, than upon the system.

> Our system [Nock writes] was founded in all good faith that universal elementary education would make a citizenry more intelligent; whereas obviously it has done nothing of the kind. The general level of intelli-gence in our citizenry stands exactly where it stood when the system was established. The promoters of our system ... did not know, and could not know, because the fact had not been determined, that the av-erage age at which the development of intelligence is arrested lies some-where between twelve and thirteen years.

But—and here you will see the connection with contrary opinions—Nock adds what he terms a "positive result" of our educational system. "If it had done nothing to raise the general level of intelligence, it had succeeded in making our citizenry more easily gullible. It tended powerfully to focus the credulousness of Homo sapiens upon the printed word, and to confirm him in the crude authoritarian or fetishistic spirit which one sees highly developed, perhaps, in the ha-bitual reader of newspapers." Because we were taught to believe what we read in our schoolbooks, and what our

[18]Harper & Brothers, 1943. See also Nock's Our Enemy The State (1930 and Letters from Albert Jay Nock (1949), The Caxton Printers, Ltd.

teachers told us, we bred the habit of "unthinking acquiescence" rather than exercising such intelligence as we may have.

This makes Homo sapiens (may be translated as "wise guy," perhaps) "an easy mark," as Nock says, "for whatever deleterious nonsense may be presented to him under the appearance of authority."

So, let us employ contrary opinions in order to avoid the errors of mass "*un*thinking" and then use common horsesense to arrive at decisions. In this way, you can "beat the game" but it is *you* who beats it, not the theory. The theory is merely a "way" of thinking—a "way" of arriving at decisions.

THINKING BY ACCIDENT

In times of befuddlement and flustration (when you're frustrated from being flustered!) —such as in recent years and likely in the foreseeable future—a large part of thinking and planning is by accident. Like the World War I aviators who flew by the seats of their pants.

National and international policies, as well as everyday business affairs, are ruled more and more by short-term events—by accident—instead of long-range planning.

The following brief paragraph from the Forrestal Diaries emphasizes this short-swing versus long-term addiction.

June 6, 194S—I am more impressed than ever as things develop in the world today that policy may be frequently shaped by events unless some one has strong and clear mental grasp of events; strong enough and clear enough so that he is able to shape policy rather than letting it be shaped by accidents. [See "Put the Cart Before the Horse," which follows.]

Now it is this writer's contention that the Theory of Contrary Opinion can be of aid in this problem of thinking and planning by accident and incident.

It seems to me that we can form the habit of asking ourselves, when some important prediction is being aired, "That may be very well for the short swing, but how will it work over the long pull?" And, vice versa.

In other words, we can be contrary to timing as well as to events. Some generally accepted opinions may be correct, we'll say, for the long future, but when examined contrarily are likely to be a delusion for the near term.

Conversely, there are frequently ideas that grasp people's minds and become imbedded there about which they cannot have *any* sound long-term opinion because of unknowable factors that will arise. One such thought comes to mind. It was not many years ago that it was generally accepted as an economic fact that the United States had reached a point of tteconomic maturity." Do you remember when we heard little else except that our economy was mature, that underconsumption was to be permanent, and unemployment constant? You heard the same fixed ideas a short two years ago about the certainty of inflation, a prolonged period of prosperity, and no recession while the government poured money into defense. By 1953 "everyone" was talking slump again.

Another way contrary thinking helps us is in avoiding the costly habit of judging the future by the present. That is, the inclination to assume that if it is sunny and warm today it will be sunny and warm tomorrow. This was illustrated in 1929, you recall, when we were perched upon a "permanent plateau of prices" for common stocks. The rise had lasted so long—it would last forever. The "New Era" sprouted from the same delusion of projecting today into tomorrow without thought of what might happen during the night.

PUT THE CART BEFORE THE HORSE

This writer believes (along with the late James Forrestal) that in our present world crisis "events control men's actions" . . . and further (admittedly somewhat cynical) that world events appear too big for men's minds to successfully cope with.

If there is any truth in these assertions, there should be an approach to this problem via the theory of contrary opinion.

It seems to me that it might well be demonstrated that in times of crisis events would always control men's actions. Without attempting to examine several crises here let us note what one great mind had to say about this at another time of perilous crisis for our nation. In a letter to A. G. Hodges, on April 4, 1864, President Lincoln commented upon his attitude toward slavery. In closing, he added this: ". . . I attempt no compliment to my own sagacity. I claim not to have controlled events, but confess plainly that events have controlled me. Now, at the end of three years' struggle, the nation's condition is not what either party, or any man, devised or expected...."

In looking back, with the advantage of historical perspective, it is generally conceded, I have no doubt, that although he did not control events President Lincoln did have the intellectual capacity and moral fortitude to cope with events and conditions as they arose and developed.

While it is obviously merely individual opinion that present men's minds do not appear capable of contending with the forces of events, nonetheless events will continue to unfold—and the leaders of nations will continue to cope with them to the best of their ability, or will cope with them in such manner as they hope will be to their best advantage.

Inasmuch as world politics directs the thinking of political leaders, the method of contending or grappling with events may be twisted in accordance with goals which a given nation's leaders may hope to attain. Realistically, therefore, one approach may be advantageous to one country while highly disadvantageous to another.

Under such complex and devious situations wherein can the theory of contrary opinion be of any assistance?

It seems to me that we have to put the cart before the horse: we have to put the event before the men (the leaders who make the decisions). We think of men leading us, as a horse draws the cart. But actually the events drag the leaders after them. In consequence, if we think first of the events, trying in our small way to analyze the events—regardless of how leaders will react to them—we then see the facts uncolored by the personalities.

It may be assumed that events will follow one another in dismaying succession. What leaders' viewpoints will be is unknown and unpredictable. We fear what Khruschev or Molotov will do. There is as much doubt of what Churchill, Rhee, Mao Tsetung, Eisenhower, or the leaders of France or Italy may do or say. Events will sway actions.

LAW OF UNIVERSAL INEQUALITY

When the social falsifiers, with their pernicious propaganda, try to make us believe that there should be full equality among everybody, let us contrary realists take heed of Pareto's Law of Universal Inequality.

Vilfredo Pareto (1848-1923) was a brilliant engineer, born in Paris of Italian parentage. His discovery of the "distribution of incomes" became known as Pareto's Law while the graphic representation of his law is known as the Pareto Curve.

According to Carl Snyder (see below) , Pareto's Law states, in simplest terms, "that the larger incomes are received by comparatively few people, the number with large incomes are more numerous, and as the incomes decrease the number receiving these lower incomes steadily increases in a very smooth curve.

"If we represent graphically by logarithms the various levels of income and the number of persons in receipt of each level of income, the 'curve' so drawn will be a straight line (with minor discrepancies at the extremes of the curve)."

Of what good is Pareto's Law? you may be asking yourself. Everyone knows there are millions more poor people than rich ones.

The basic concept that is so important in this law is that those nations which have developed the largest wealthy classes also have the highest standard of living among *all* the population. A moment's re-. flection on the comparison between, say, China and the United States will emphasize this.

Moreover, any long-run *lowering* of the incomes of the top groups will *decrease* the incomes of those all the way down to the bottom. Perhaps it would be clearer to say that any shrinkage in the large-income groups would cause a lowering of the standard of living of the groups below. (Short-run income decreases, due to temporary heavy taxation, are not considered.)

So, when the social experimenters talk to you about equalizing incomes you can turn to Pareto's Law and demonstrate that if incomes are equalized they will be equalized at *low* levels—and, further, that as time passes the standard of living will sink to the levels of those nations which have relatively few rich.

> General welfare is derived *from* more crumbs falling off the *increasing numbers* of wealthy tables; not by taking away the tables and making everybody eat at a trough.

Now, to refer back to Carl Snyder. For many years he was the econoinic statistician of the Federal Reserve Bank of New York and an outstanding writer and thinker on economic subjects. His contributions to economic science were noteworthy. His magnum opus was a penetrating (but de-

[19]New York: The Macmillan Company, 1940.

lightfully written) book entitled *Capitalism the Creator.*[19] This is a book that every student of new isms and delusions keeps at his bedside for stimulation and sound sleep. Snyder's chapter on Pareto is illuminating and it explains the statistical findings that have substantiated Parcto's discovery.

PROPAGANDA

So long as the international tension lasts we are going to be more and more submerged in "propagandized" news. Wc shall need to reach for contrary opinions to keep from being drowned.

Suppose we take a brief look at propaganda "devices" and also wherein, it seems to me, we and the Russians are diainetrically opposed.

If we are to arrive at some comprehension of the uses of propaganda we first have to try and determine what Russia wants and what the Western nations want.

1. First, let's consider Russia ...
   a. Russia requires a crisis in order to control her citizenry and prevent a revolt of the masses.
   b. Without a continuing crisis it is a fair assumption that Russia would collapse because dictatorships must llave an excuse for regimenting the people.
2. Now look at our side ..
   a. We wish to get rid of the crisis in order to avoid collapse.
   b. Western nations are sickly worried that a major war may result.
   c. If the crisis persists too long Western nations will face collapse. (Great Britain, France, and other countries are already about at the end of their ropes and must be bolstered).

You can see that propaganda is going to be used quite differently by Russia from the manner in which the 'Western nations will use it.

Clyde R. Miller, in his book, *The Process of Persuasion*,[20] lists what he terms the "four simple devices" employed to achieve the acceptance or rejection of ideas or beliefs.

1. The Acceptance or "Virtue" Device . . . designed to cause us to accept by association with "good" words, symbols, acts.

   The Rejection or "Poison" Device . . . to cause us to reject by association with "bad" words, symbols, acts.

   The Testimonial Device . . accept or reject according to "good" or "bad."

1. The "Together" Device . . . to cause us to accept or reject by the application of any or all devices applied through the pressure of group or mass emotion and action.

Referring to the disarmament proposals, by way of example, wc note that the "virtue" device employed by us is, of course, the good idea of "peace." Vishinsky's tirades in 1951-52 against the TrumanAcheson proposal employed the "poison" (and ridicule) device to the limit. Vishinsky's "bad" word is warmonger (reiterated over and over), which he applies to the Western powers at every opportunity. Not wishing to appear against peace, however, the Soviet Foreign Minister made a counterproposal for a four-power conference on disarmament, as you doubtless recall.

Note the Russian pattern of propaganda right up to Malenkov's hydrogen-bomb speech in August, 1953. It is two-edged: peaceful solution of all world problems, except for the war philosophy of the United States.

---

[20]New York: Crown Publishers, 1946. Study it, by all means.

From this brief look at the art of propaganda I think you will agree that contrary thinking will prove valuable in seeing through propaganda.

REALISM: THE CONTRARY CHALLENGE OF THE NEW YEAR

This was written in December, as you will see.

With Christmas over, we in the country hang up a new calendar in the kitchen and wonder what the New Year will bring forth. There is something stimulating about throwing an old calendar away. A fresh start is good for sluggish minds.

This challenge is before us each year's end: Let us make contrary thinking more intelligible, more coherent, more convincing. We all know full well that there is much to be learned about the art of *contrary* thinking.

You may have noticed, of late, references in the writings of others to contrary opinions. So perhaps a repetition of this writer's concept of the theory of contrary opinions is not out of place.

> The basic usefulness of contrary thinking lies in its objective and realistic approach. Contrary thinking enables one to fight shy of personal opinions and preconceived opinions; of hopes and wishful thinking; of leaps to conclusions and mass sentiment.
>
> Realism will indeed be essential in *every* New Year.

A primary shortcoming of the Theory of Contrary Opinion might be mentioned:

Nothing is more common to find in economic writing than the habit of upholding previously expressed opinions.

In the use of contrary opinions it is a great temptation to force opposite viewpoints in order to support *personal* opinions. If a person has pre-established views on an economic trend he is likely to turn to contrary opinions merely for corroboration. Unless he is unusually well disciplined mentally he will center his attention on those opinions which he can twist around to confirm his previous conclusions.

Let us adopt a policy of avoiding personal opinions we have to uphold! If, for example, one is forthright in making predictions and rendering advice, he cannot objectively evaluate opinions and sentiment. He cannot escape supporting his advices and predictions.

I believe it to be a true psychological fact that one cannot be objective and at the same time render advice. You cannot be personal and impersonal at the same time. When one offers advice his mind is naturally focussed on "hoping" to make the advice come right, rather than on the objective and realistic viewpoints that might influence the advices.

This writer believes there is room among the voluminous printings of forecasts and dopesheets for comments that discuss what others are predicting, advising, and "opinionating." You then can make up your own mind. In the final analysis, every person is his own best adviser and must accept the responsibility for his decisions.

HOW ECONOMISTS SOMETIMES MAKE
THEIR PREDICTIONS GO WRONG

You may think that this writer is critical of the predictions of others. Let me assure you that it is never my intent to appear as a critic, when some comment of mine is presented that is contrary to the united predictions of economists and financial commentators. This group of responsible professionals is held in the highest regard. I read their comments and analyses with care. I dare to say I read them with more attention than is generally accorded their views, because "being contrary" requires it.

However, this brings up an intriguing side light to economic forecasting: the *influence* of economic forecasters that sometimes makes their predictions go wrong.

In the past twenty years the field for professional economists and analysts has widened enormously. Today numerous corporations have economic departments, when only a few years ago this was almost unheard of. The old-time industrialists and businessmen had little use for what they referred to as "longhaired theorists." These rugged individualists figured no one could tell them anything about their business or their future. They'd make their own futures, by the Lord Harry—and many of them did, too!

The result of this shift to economists in the ranks of business and of government, to the growth of economic services, to the voluminous dope and statistics in magazines and "Letters," has been that at

giAien time you may find literally hundreds of predictions appearing in print and being aired over radiotelevision.

And, every so often, strange as it may seem, these predictions and analyses sound so much alike that you wonder if the gentlemen haven't joined up and worked over their ideas, by give and take, until all agree.

When this occurs it obviously is going to have a heavy influence on business minds and upon the minds of the public. A businessman is going to be impressed, when he picks up his newspaper or magazine, and sees that eighty, or two hundred, economists see eye to eye on what's likely to happen.

It is not that the many are wrong in their analyses, *but that they may be proven wrong because of their influence.* They may so affect operations and plans of business (and of the public) that their forecasts fail to prove out. If you are convinced that inflation is going to accelerate you will manage your inventories and bank loans differently from what you would if you had been led to expect a slump. Collective action, from united predictions, often pushes the pendulum too far in one direction—thus upsetting the "timing" and the momentum previously expected. Just as overloading will throw a machine out of gear, so will an overweight (of one-way action) throw the economy out of gear.

So it is that economists may see their published predictions go wrong whereas if they had kept them secret the forecasts might well have worked out with extraordinary accuracy.

ASK "WHAT'S RIGHT?"—INSTEAD OF ALWAYS "WHAT'S WRONG?"

Have you noticed the tendency we all have of immediately asking "What's wrong?" when some economic or political question comes up for discussion? You can think of any number of examples:

> If arguing about the general business situation, someone is sure to ask: "What's wrong with business today, anyway?"
> Or, about the stock market: Brokers are asked over and over, every day—"What's wrong with the market?" Did you ever hear anyone inquire, "What's right with the market?"

Yet I'll venture to assert that if you ask what's right about economic trends, when you're thinking about them, you will get an entirely fresh slant on things. Your mind will travel in different channels. Try it sometime—indeed, make it a habit. It is a contrary habit much to be recommended.

The negative approach to socio-economic questions has become a fixation.

People have developed what psychologists and doctors refer to as "the depression phychosis" or the looking-for-trouble habit. Bring up almost any question about domestic or foreign affairs—and you will hear voices at once chime in that "it won't work," "it can't be done," and so on. It re-

minds one of the horse-and-buggy days when Henry Ford
and the other horseless-carriage inventors were scoffed at.

This reminds me of an interesting example of
thinking right which is related in the book, Watch
Your Margin. A smart investor was riding in one of
the early twolungers, and after a speedy fifteen-mile-
san-hour spin inquired what made the contraption
run. When told it was gasoline, he at once bought
himself a bundle of Mr. Rockefeller's certificates.
He knew that Standard Oil would sell its product
and stay in business, and he also figured a lot of the
early-bird manufacturers of autos would drop by
the wayside. So, by asking himself what was right
about the gas buggies—and not worrying about
what was wrong—he made a future killing.

It seems to me that if we are to ride through the next
decade without losing our sense of balanceand are to enjoy
any sort of contentment in lifewe need to dwarf our trou-
bles and magnify our blessings.

If we start asking "What's right?" about this or that question we shall find we are actually changing our whole
method of thinking. Heaven knows we don't enjoy figuring
the fiendish taxes of today, but it wasn't so long ago that
you and I both probably were thinking that *anything*, even
killing taxes, would be better than a runaway inflation. Obviously, I'll agree that taxes can be too high (they are now,
from an economic standpoint) but perhaps if students concentrated on what is the *right* amount we might solve the
problem.

MASS PSYCHOLOGY AND THE CAMPAIGNS

One could write a book on crowd psychology and use the 1952 Republican campaigns for the nomination for the illustrations. It would include every rule in the game for leading and misleading the crowd. One contender swung the sledge hammer to gain and hold attention. The other gained ground through the emotional appeals via suggestion, imagination, contagion.

Students of crowd psychology know that the average voter pays scant attention to the fundamental facts concerning either the candidate or the platform. He accepts "what he feels." The forces of suggestibility and contagion form the image in his mind.

Mystery is an all-powerful tool. "Tell 'em nothing and promise 'em anything," counsels the politician; "and, above all, never reason with voters; affirm but never explain; repeat what you'll do for 'em, but never argue."

The principles of winning the crowd gave General Eisenhower the breaks early in 1952. Far off in Paris, it was a simple matter to build him up as a great idol. Being aloof from the rough and tough campaigning he retained glamour and fascination. His supporters here at home worked on the emotions of the people by constantly strumming their theme of "leadership," "popularity," and "only Ike can win." Avoiding arguments, they played on the heart strings, forcing the late Senator Taft into the tough spot of winning the minds.

The silly slogan, "I Like Ike," shows how the propaganda was brought down to the level of a school child. "I like Ike and that's enough; what more do you want?" It was brutally simple, difficult to defeat, and highly contagious.

In the meantime, Taft had to exert constant pressure just to keep before the public. He could not let up for an instant. Lacking full press support (indeed most of it was for the General) , he had to press his own support. The opposition's claim that "Taft can't win" was a devastating slogan that he had to combat. (Nothing could be harder to oppose. What a sly and clever stroke that was!)

Thus the contest stood when Eisenhower returned.

The question remained whether Eisenhower could win the election if he were nominated. He would then be out in the arena. The public would learn that he wasn't as perfect as the image. People would take sides, and be disappointed in some of his views. As I wrote at the time, if the General followed the guides of mass psychology—saying little and assuring much; and repeating it—he could probably win out over Stevenson. But if he started to argue and appealed to reason, the smart Democrats would snow him under. They never explain anything, but promise everything (I'm speaking of New Deal Democrats now) . That is what wins the majority. (See " 'Crowd Upset' Favors Eisenhower," page 101, which was written just prior to the election.)

SOCIAL PSYCHOLOGY

In view of the fundamental question of the appeal of Communism to many minds, it might be well for us to consider psychological aspects of the socioeconomic trends.

> Primarily, the clash between socialism and capitalism is a competition between hearts and minds; between wishes and logic; between appeals to emotions and appeals to reason.

No more provocative book, I dare say, has been written on this subject than Gustave Le Bon's *The Psychology of Socialism*. It was published in 1899— many years before more than a passing thought was given to state socialism in this country. Now out of print and quite scarce, it is as up-to-date as today's newspaper. Suppose we quote from it briefly. In the Preface (keeping in mind the book was written fifty-four years ago) Le Bon said this:

> If we would comprehend the profound influence of modern Socialism we need only to examine its doctrines. . . . Like religions (and Socialism is tending more and more to put on the guise of a religion) it propagates itself in any manner than by reason. Feeble in the extreme when it attempts to reason, and to support itself by economic arguments, it becomes on the contrary extrem* powerful when it remains in the region of dreams, affirmations, and chimerical promises. . . . Now the great power of beliefs, when they tend to assume this religious form . . . lies in the fact that their propagation is independent of the proportion of truth or error they may contain, for as soon as a belief has gained a lodging in the minds of men its absurdity no longer appears; reason cannot reach it, and only time can impair it. . .

Now, jumping all the way to the back of the book (of 415 pages), note the following from Le Bon's summary and "Future of Socialism":

> The individual is nothing to Socialism . . . Psychology, on the contrary, teaches us that as soon as the individual makes part of a crowd he loses the greater part of the mental qualities which constitute his strength. . . . Associations of workers on the one hand and employers on the other hand are able to fight on an equal footing, which the individual could not do. This is doubtless only the substitution of collective for individual autocracy, and we have no reason for calling the first less severe than the second. Indeed, the contrary is sufficiently evident. . . . Social upheavals are commenced always from above, never from below. . . . Herbert Spencer is no less gloomy. The triumph of Socialism, he says, vvould be the greatest disaster the world has ever known, and the end of it would be military despotism. . . . Let us remember that history shows us that popular movements are in reality only the movement of a few leaders; let us remember the simplicism of crowds . . . and, finally, the mechanism of those elements of persuasion which I attempted to present in a preceding volume [*The Crowd*[21]]— affirmation, repetition, contagion, and prestige.

ECONOMIC PSYCHOLOGY

The aim of this writer's contrary comments is to proffer interpretations in the field of economic psychology, still largely unexplored. One does not find, for example, the title "Economic Psychologist" used as yet. The few -writers who are paying serious attention to the study of human behaviorism and its influence upon economic trends refer to themselves as sociologists, economists, or psychologists.

---

[21]*The Crowd; A Study of the Popular Mind*—Le Bon's popular book—is now available in a paper-back edition, by Viking Press, N.Y.

However, it is evident from studies and papers presented in recent years—and from the surveys of consumer intentions and attitudes which have been conducted for the Federal Reserve Board—that the field of economic psychology is one in which serious concentration will be focussed in coming years.

In *Psychological Analysis of Economic Behavior*,[22] Professor George Katona asserts that "economic developments without regard to people's perceptions of them and reactions to them do not suffice for a full understanding of cyclical fluctuations."

This, of course, is the running theme of our discussions. It is not enough for us to know the statistical setup of the moment—or even the probable statistical *outlook*. We need more importantly (1) to know how consumers and businessmen look upon (react to) these statistical reports and probabilities, and (2) we then need to consider a contrary opinion on trends thus commonly accepted.

Perhaps one of the significant facts one learns as he studies this new "science" of economic psychology is that factors which influence people at one time may have little effect upon them at another.

Also, it may be said that people tend to remember the most recent similar experience, and are prone to forget causes with a different result of a prior time. Because of the pronounced postwar depression during 1920-21, there was general expectancy fot a similar severe slump after World War II. Yet, looking back, one notes it was entirely overlooked that a wild boom and inflation took place (1919)

---

[22]McGraw-HUI Book Company, Inc., 1951.

before the postwar depression and deflation occurred. Moreover, it is informative to recall that the inflation-boom of 1919 was universally *unanticipated,* an immediate slump then being predicted as it was in 1945-46.

Today, we are beginning to be fed economic nostrums that are reminiscent of former eras. We are told, for instance, that there need never be another full-fledged economic depression. Some observers state categorically that there will never be a repetition of 1930-33. In other times similar claims have employed other references, such as the statement that there would never be another "1873," or another panic like "1893."

So, while we cannot foretell the future, we can be confident that economic psychology will be a required subject for study as we learn more about economic trends and cycles—and what starts and stops them.

LOOKING BACK

As election news was predominant during 1952 I thought at the time it might be interesting to turn to another year of a hot contest-1884, between Blaine and Cleveland. Economic conditions had a strong influence, as they usually do have. In addition, there was a widespread revolt against the "sins" of the Republicans. Corruptive practices were pinned on the party in power, and Blaine himself did not escape severe censure.

Perhaps one of the surprising things about those days was the lack of political news in the strictly financial press. I ran through the fifty-two issues of the *Financial and Commercial Chronicle* for 1884 and failed to find any mention of the campaign until in the early autumn, at which time it was remarked that betting odds were five to four on Blaine. Just before the election the paper reported the odds had switched to five to four on Cleveland. (The latter won by the slimmest of margins.)

The year 1884 witnessed a severe (but brief) stockmarket panic, and slumping business conditions with many failures. The failure of the brokerage firm of Grant & Ward was notorious, as the former President and Union Army hero was involved, although guiltlessly. (General Grant thereupon wrote his famous *Personal Memoirs* to pay off the huge debt caused by Ward's crookedness.)

Pessimism was rampant during the spring, summer, and fall of 1884 (aiding Cleveland's election) and yet, looking back, one sees that this was the bottom of the relatively brief depression. The stock market started a persistent climb which—although at first "doubted," as all initial recoveries are doubted—lasted, with moderate interruptions, until the major depression of 1893 set in. Industrial and trade activity also recovered from their slumps and good business was had until 1893. Thus a side light on a former political battle when feeling ran high.

While on the subject of elections, let me leave with you a thought on the contrary-opinion theory and elections: When you think of 1948 you might jump to conclusions and assume that being contrary is smart thinking in an election year.

The great majority of elections are either so close that opinions are balanced, or so one-sided that general opinions have been correct. For example, it would have been silly to have been "opposite" to Hoover's chances in 1928, or Roosevelt's in 1936.

The 1948 election stands by itself, I think. It was a pollster's fiasco and cannot be considered as a "normal" election condition.

AN HISTORIC RETURN TO GOLD

Because of the growing interest in sound money versus the skidding dollar of recent years, it is informative to turn back to another era when the United States left the gold standard—and to note the contrary occurrence when we returned to gold in 1879.

In February, 1862, the first issue of "greenbacks" was released. We deserted the gold standard "to finance the war" and did not return for seventeen years. (It is now about twenty years since F.D.R. took us off gold for the second time.) Greenbacks fluctuated wildly, sinking at one time to thirty-three cents in terms of gold. Parity with gold was not reached until December 17, 1878—a fortnight before "resumption" of the gold standard was to be effected.

There were widespread fears as the resumption date of January 2, 1879, drew near. Many expected to see a "run" on gold, with greenbacks piled counterhigh in banks as people demanded gold for their paper dollars.

All fears were groundless. Contrary to the expectations of many groups the government actually *gained* gold on the first day of resumption. When folks found they could get the gold, they didn't want it! Paper was easier to carry in their pockets. This report from the *New York. Tribune,* of Friday, January 3, 1879, gives us a "feel" of the times:

Resumption of specie payments was formally accomplished yesterday. The United States Sub-Treasury could not get rid of gold, and its receipts exceeded payments by $268,000. . . . • The event was celebrated by a National salute and the display of flags from Government and financial buildings.

On Saturday, January 4, the *Commercial and Financial Chronicle* commented that the nation had "quietly passed into a new commercial condition."

> Thus closes the history of war finances [added the *Chronicle*]. It is useless to say at this time that these issues [the greenbacks] were unnecessary, that the nation might have conducted the war without paying so dearly for it. All we are interested in knowing today is that, having been issued, and having passed through the various stages of depreciation with constant fluctuation for 17 years, we are at length once again safely anchored upon a fixed standard and subject in all respects to the universal law of value. ... .

Next worry was the fear that an outflow of gold to Europe would exhaust the reserves to a point where free convertibility might be in doubt. The recovery in security prices in the first half year of 1879 invited selling of American securities by foreign holders. This took gold across the ocean. However, fortuitous circumstances saved the situation for the United States. While our grain crops were the largest on record, those of England, France, Austria, Germany, and Russia were the poorest in years. Our huge supplies of grains saved Europe from famine—and, at the same time, reversed the flow of gold. This assured the success of resumption. With rising prices and renewed confidence, general activity set in which carried forward with a welcome burst of prosperity. Revival from the long depression of 1873-78 was thus abetted by "gold."

CONTRARY EVENTS FROM HISTORY

In studying the art of contrary thinking it is useful to review history.

For example, the following, with the change of a word or two (which we've done in parentheses) , reads as if it were taken from a business magazine in our recent election year of 1952:

Optimism is the rule of the market. This is the season for optimism, just as February is the season for pessimism; and besides, the market has much in its favor that, season or no season, optimism would still be the rule. In addition to the big war (defense) orders, there is the cheapness of money, the soundness of the banking situation, and big demand for all goods and commodities. . . .

Seldom have the security markets been in a better position in a political year. They have had something to gain and nothing to lose; for they may be helped to a moderate extent by a more favorable attitude toward big business, whereas they can scarcely be hurt at all, at least for the next few years, by anything that may be done to the tariff (defense and foreign-aid program). . . .

The above was taken from John Moody's "Review of the Financial Markets," which appeared in the November, 1916, issue of *Moody's Magazine*.

From a contrary standpoint it is informative to note that it was in November, 1916, that the stock market registered the high point of the "war market" —to the surprise of observers. Profits, yields, and business activity, were at extraordinary peaks. War orders from the Allies reached stupendous figures for that era. (It was a great era: money was borrowed from us in the hundreds of millions and then spent here for munitions and war equipment.)

The summer that had just passed witnessed the rather colorless political campaign between Wilson and Hughes. It was a close race. Some older readers may recall that on the morning after election day Judge Hughes was thought to be the victor, but late returns from California turned the tables and Wilson was re-elected.

Persistently, in the face of enormous war business and huge profits, the stock market continued in a bear-market trend for thirteen months. Our declaration of war in April, 1917, did not deter the trend; it gained momentum downward, particularly in the second half of the year.

During 1916 there were wishful beliefs that Germany would lose the war shortly. Peace overtures were made from time to time. This was blamed for the market's decline— after the decline was well under way. Yet, when the market started back up again, in December, 1917, it actually kept on going up until the day of the Armistice (November 11, 1918). Then, after a setback of roughly 10 per cent, stocks took off again on the fly for the 1919 bull market and inflationary binge, just when "everyone" was sure there'd be an immediate postwar bust.

TIDAL MOVEMENTS

Contrarians are profoundly concerned with "tidal movements" and "waves" of public opinion and public hysteria. The manias of mankind have been motivated and kept in motion by these tidal waves of emotions.

You are familiar with the stories of manias, and

with books which relate them, from the previous section of this pamphlet. But let me lump together a few books that contain the narratives of manias and the background of public psychology as reflected in manias and in "tidal movements." Not all of the following are in print, but several should be obtainable in libraries.

Memoirs of Extraordinary Popular Delusions and the Madness of Crowds, by Charles Mackay. (Reprinted by Farrar, Straus Bc Cudahy, Inc., N.Y.; available from Fraser Publishing Co., Wells, Vt.).

The Crowd—A Study of the Popular Mind, by Gustave Le Bon. (Available from Fraser Publishing Co., Wells, Vt.)

The Psychology of Socialism, by Gustave Le Bon. (Hard to find.)

Instincts of the Herd in Peace and War, by William Trotter.

The Laws of Imitation, by Gabriel Tarde. (Scarce, but in some libraries.)

Psychological Analysis of Economic Behavior, by Professor George Katona. (The McGraw-Hill Book Company, Inc.)

Perpetual War for Perpetual Peace, edited by Dr. Harry Elmer Barnes, in collaboration with seven other outstanding contributors. (The Caxton Printers, Ltd., 1953.) This book is recommended reading for contrarians as it portrays in a devastating and fully documented manner the power of modern propaganda. It is a *revisionist* history of the past sixteen years, and it clearly demonstrates how essential it is to examine contrarily the accepted socio-political beliefs, ideologies, and propaganda.

There are others, of course, but the first five, above, give you the fundamentals of mass manias and mass psychology. Katona's book analyzes economic behavior from the standpoint of consumers (Professor Katona has directed the consumer surveys for the Federal Reserve Board) .

It is unquestionably the . . . what shall I say? . . . the "duty" of contrary-minded people like ourselves to dig into this question of "tidal movements" because it is quite evident a wave of "internationalism" has engulfed public thought in this country. Therefore, we of the minority thought should give the question more consideration and analysis than is commonly given in order to arrive at correct answers—and perhaps to influence others if we judge they are being carried away on the "waves."

MUCH TO LEARN

As we go along with the study of the Theory of Contrary Opinion we find that we have much to learn about its *application*.

> *When* to be contrary? What *intensity* of general opinions should we look for? How to measure opinions?

These are a few of the questions always confronting us. However, we need not be too discouraged, it seems to me, because the whole field of economics remains a "guessy" one. Little, if any, progress has been made over the years in attaining profitable accuracy in economic forecasting. And, mind you, this condition still exists, notwithstanding the extraordinary volume of statistics that is now available to students and which was not known to former forecasters.

It seems to me that the long history of economic forecasting clearly demonstrates that "psychology" is the missing key. You may have all the statistics in the world at your finger tips, but still you do not know how or when people are going to act. Accordingly, the statistics frequently lead you astray. Long years ago John Stuart Mill said that "crisis is not a matter of the purse, but of the mind." You will find among the old writers on economics that occasionally someone ascribed "changing conditions to varying mental moods," as Senator Theodore E. Burton did in his grand book published in 1902 *(Financial Crisis and Periods of Industrial and Commercial Depressions)*, which I have referred to previously.[23]

Speaking of Burton's book, let me select from it a few examples which will show when a "contrary opinion" would have been quite useful.

In July, 1825, for example, the King's Speech (as read by the Lord Chancellor) was congratulating the Parliament on the opening of the session, referring to the "general and increasing prosperity . . . that continues to pervade every part of his kingdom." A financial crisis occurred in December—five months later.

On March 15, 1873, the London Economist wrote glowingly of the developments throughout Europe which augured for a bright outlook. In less than two months—May 9, 1873—the Bourse at Vienna closed "and a crisis of great severity occurred, followed by a depression of exceptional length." (Later in the year, the great American crisis and depression of 1873 set in.)

On December 31, 1892, R. G. Dun 8c Company's *Weekly Review of Trade* said: "The most prosperous year ever known in business closes today with strongly favourable indications for the future." In May, 1893, five months later, the long depression commenced which was also long remembered.

We might go on with additional similar references, but they are unnecessary.

---

[23]New York: D. Appleton and Company, Copyright 1902.

Let us end with this comment of Burton's which is worth remembering: "Crises and depressions have occurred almost contemporaneously in different countries, under every prevalent system of banking; in monarchies and republics; in countries with free trade and protective tariffs; in those having only metallic money, and in those having metallic and paper money, in those having irredeemable paper money . . . they have likewise occurred at different times in the same country, under all the various regulations adopted."

Yes, we have much to learn!

ON PREDICTING THE UNPREDICTABLE

A basic usefulness of contrary opinions is to guard against predicting the unpredictable; or, to put it another way, to avoid being ensnared by faulty *general* predictions. Having concentrated for many years on the study of the Theory of Contrary Opinion (and having put my thoughts on paper) , I believe it is correct to say that the theory is more valuable in *avoiding* errors in forecasting than in employing it for definitive forecasting.

Let me call your attention to a particularly worthwhile article that appeared a year or so ago in *The Freeman*. It was by Dr. L. Albert Hahn, an economist widely known here and in Europe. The title of the article was "Predicting the Unpredictable."

Reviewing the "wrong" forecasts of recent years (the postwar bust and deflation, then the continu-ation of inflation, etc.) , Dr. Hahn commented: "Clearly the regularity of these errors in forecasting can not be pure chance.

Something like a Law of the Necessity of Errors in Forecasting must be at work." He then added this:

It is seldom realized that belief in the possibility of "scientific" business forecasts, and the forecasting mania of our time, are comparatively
new phenomena. Until about 1930 serious econo¬mists were not so
bold—or so na'ive—as to pretend to be able to calculate the coming
of booms and depressions in advance. It would not have fitted into
their general view of the working of a free economy. They considered
the economic future as basically dependent on unpredictable price-cost
relationships and on the equally unpredictable psychological reactions
of entre¬preneurs. Predictions of future business conditions would
have seemed to them mere charlatanry, just as predictions, say,
regard¬ing the resolutions of Congress two years from now.

The forecasting mania of our era (and the assured usefulness of contrary opinions, if I may interpolate) stems in
Dr. Hahn's view from "Keynesian economics."

The basic error of the whole (Keynesian) approach [says Hahn] lies
in the fact that the causative link between objective data and the decision of the members of the community are treated as mechanical. But
men are still men and not automatons....
Forecasting the economic future means forecasting decisions on investment and consumption that are as uncertain as the whole future ...
What leads to the maldistribution of demand—called the business
cycle—is that the majority of entrepreneurs are at times too optimistic
or too pessimistic; that they either invest too much and too soon, or
too little and too late. . . .

Let me add one or two more pungent sayings by this
clear-thinking economist: "Calculated depressions do not
happen. Nor, by the way, do calculated inflations—though
it was so popular, just before the latest recession in com-
modity prices [1951] to calculate a new inflation in advance.
A recession [in prices] was clearly due the moment theorists

began to speak of our age as the age of permanent inflation. ..."

"CROWD UPSET" FAVORS EISENHOWER

[This essay, ivritten in October, 1952, is included for its reference to the use of contrary opinions in an election campaign.]

With the election only a matter of days off, perhaps we should discuss again the thought that contrary opinions are not of important value in guessing election outcomes.

The 1948 election will be brought up at once, because in 1948 a contrary opinion most certainly *was* the correct guess. However, the writer looks upon the experience of four years ago as a "pollsters' fluke" and therefore not to be considered as an ordinary occurrence.

Generally speaking, you will find that national elections fall into two categories: (1) a contest, the outcome of which is a foregone conclusion; therefore a contrary opinion would be wrong guessing merely for the sake of being contrary; or (2) a contest so close that it is a tossup until the last who will win; in which instance there would be no general viewpoint to be contrary to.

For example, when one points to 1948 as an argument for being contrary to general opinions on elections, you can refer him at once to 1928 when Hoover's election was a general opinion—and a correct one.

Turning to this year's hotly contested and hotworded campaigns, there are two or three suppositions that might be interesting to hold in mind until November 5, but which cannot be termed as election forecasts.

There is a condition prevailing this autumn that is "new"—or at least it is thought to be new; but inasmuch as there were no "polls" in the majority of past elections we can only conjecture that the condition is new.

The new condition I refer to is the large proportion of voters who, according to the polls, are thought still to be "undecided." The undecided vote is estimated to range from one-fourth to one-third of the votes to be cast.

If we roughly (and inaccurately) break down the votes expected to be cast, they may run about like this: One third Stevenson, one third Eisenhower, and one third "haven't decided." (To repeat, this is doubtless inaccurate, but perhaps off by only a few percentage points in each segment of the voting population.)

Accordingly, there may be a great mass of voters that will swing in one direction or the other.

From our studies of mass psychology we learn that frequently a mass movement occurs which at the time is incomprehensible. Why large groups of people move as a herd is one of those traits of human nature which is difficult to decipher.

However, a mass movement is a result of emotional motivation, not of reasoning. The "crowd" is influenced by the heart (emotions) , not by the mind.

From all this it is a plausible conjecture that the "undecided mass" may move in one (composite) direction. Now I do not mean that every person will act as his neighbor does; there will be some who decide on cold analysis (perhaps) . But the great majority may jump to the same conclusion by November 4 [1952].

If an emotional movement of this kind does materialize, either candidate may win by a "landslide" —and thus the "general opinion" of a close election will be wrong.

It has been the writer's belief that the Democrats had all the advantage in emotional appeals; but that General Eisenhower does have one outstanding chance to gain the hearts of the undecided voters: namely, by concentrating on Korea.

I think this viewpoint was borne out in Eisenhower's Detroit speech ("I shall go to Korea"). The impact of this Korean address was electric and if it is followed up this week could be the spark to move the undecided mass in one direction (toward the General—but I felt a glaring slip at Detroit: no reference to MacArthur).

When one speaks of a "landslide" he might mean a landslide in the popular vote or in the Electoral C.,ollege vote. The popular vote may not differ by many millions and yet the electoral vote prove out as a landslide. So it is that the movement of the undecided mass could have surprising results.

Obviously, this mass movement can go in Stevenson's direction as well as in Eisenhower's favor. And perhaps it will; but it seems to me that if the election outcome is to prove a surprise it will be an overwhelming victory for Eisenhower.

The odds of analysis and experience favor Stevenson, whereas the possibility of a "crowd upset" seems to be a long shot on the General.

MONEY MINDS

The invincible success of American capitalism rests upon an unbeatable formula:

Money-making minds plus engineering genius equals constant growth.

On the (hopeful) assumption that freedom to make money will have its shackles removed, suppose we look briefly at "money minds." When money minds are restrained and restricted, constant growth is impeded.

Pick any community you wish—from a farming hamlet, through small and large cities, up to metropolitan centers—and you will find a tiny minority of money-makers. Nature has been frugal in dispensing this aptitude, but has seen to it that it appears sparingly within groups wherever situated. Thus ttgrowth" may spread evenly.

Money-making is a mental characteristic. It is my personal belief that it is an exceedingly difficult art to acquire; that, indeed, one is born with it. You have an acquisitive nature (I believe) , or you haven't.

With those who have the natural aptitude for money-making it makes little difference whether "conditions" are rising, falling, or stabilizing. Their minds grasp opportunities to make money; which is to say that they have the faculty of making their opportunities. They may lose everything through overspeculation, but they are quick to make a comeback (until age dulls the mental characteristics that have to do with money) .

Education has little or nothing to do with the money-making characteristic. You have known and have read about numerous men who were ignorant from a schooling stand-point, who have amassed fortunes. (A good many of the Robber Barons, whom the "liberals" are always harping about, come within this category of "uneducated" money-makers.)

Thousands of people have made money, of course, who haven't this instinct. A few inventors (but the really wealthy ones had a money-making quirk in their make-up) and men of extraordinary capabilities whose skills have commanded large fees and salaries, come within these groups. Also en-tertainers, until popularity fades.

Equality in money-making, as in other undertakings and professions, is beyond the reach of nature. Superior abilities of all types are in the minority. Gustave Le Bon (in *The Psychology of Peoples*) says "history shows that it is to the circum-scribed elite that we owe all the advances made." He then adds this reminder: "If we allow ourselves to be too much blinded by our dreams of universal equality we shall be the first victims of our attitudes. Equality carries inferiority in its wake. .. .."

To many the idea of concentrated money-making is re-pugnant. Their interests lie in other directions. This is for-tunate, indeed, or we would not have enjoyed the fruits of the great minds of history which have given us wisdom, beauty, and culture.

However, purely from the viewpoint of economic ag-grandizement—and the general social welfare—it is fortu-nate that nature has endowed a few minds with the money-making instinct, for without it America would not be able to "rescue" the world as we now are endeavoring to do. Let us be thankful for the minority that is endowed with superior attributes. Those of us who lack them can strive to copy!

WHY FORECASTS GO HAYWIRE

Making predictions has become a mania. Practically all economists are called upon for their future views—and many go out of their way to write articles and make speeches about "what's ahead." You hear all manner of theories proposed and presented.

But the significant fact for us to hold before us is that the more prominence predictions receive the more inaccurate they are likely to be.

You might say that "predicting" has received official blessing and support when you consider the forecasting bureau that has been established by congressional authority, namely, the President's Council of Economic Advisers. This bureau is required to issue annual reports concerning the outlook, and in the past has issued them more frequently. (Under President Eisenhower there will be far less public predicting, apparently.)

We have seen the science of forecasting pass through various stages as this or that "theory" has come into the spotlight. Remember how Lord Keynes and Keynesianism were most talked about only a short time back? Today there seems to be a leaning toward mathematics and slide rules, the factors being analyzed in an engineering manner. And so it goes: everyone constantly hunting for the key to the future.

However, it would appear that composite predictions by authoritative forecasters can never prove out because their acceptance will be their downfall.

If you believe the predictions, you act against them to protect yourself. Thus, you help the predictions to go haywire.

I think I am on safe ground in asserting that so long as predictions remain popular, and are so numerous as they are today—and so long as they receive notoriety through repetition in the press and on the radio—*contrary opinions will increase in importance as thinking aids.*

REVOLUTIONS REQUIRE THE LONG VIEW

Because of the wishful hopes which are commonly expressed today concerning revolts in Russiancontrolled countries, it seems a good time to read up a little on revolutions and what makes them tick. One of the principles of contrary thinking is to avoid -wishful thinking and preconceived opinions.

I think we can start with the assertion that the masses will only revolt to free themselves from some form of tyranny. People will not rise up to subjugate themselves further.

Secondly, there appears to be some relationship in time between the years during which the masses have been under a regime which has enslaved or harrassed them, and the time it takes them to become sufficiently aroused (and organized) to revolt. The seeds of our American revolution, as an example, were planted long years prior to the Boston Tea Party and the battles of Concord and Lexington.

In this connection, let me refer again to Gustave Le Bon, this time to his book, *The Psychology of Revolution,*[24] which has this to say about the time element of "true" revolutions:

---

24 New York: G. P. Putman's Sons, 1915.

"The true revolutions, those which transform the destinies of the peoples, are most frequently accomplished so slowly that the historians can hardly point to their beginnings. The term evolution is, therefore, far more appropriate than revolution."

There are numerous brief *coup d'états* that have no further basis than the desire of a man or a clique to take over a government. But many of these collapse as quickly as they commence. They are not revolutions in the sense we are talking about.

It would seem highly improbable that a quick *coup d'états* would be attempted in Russia because of the long and securely intrenched police-and-security system.

Insofar as a "true" revolution is concerned, we have to remember two pertinent factors, as I see it:

1. The fact that the present system is nearly a generation old; it has a life of about thirty-five years behind it. In consequence, the doctrines and beliefs arc well established. Millions of Russians know no other system of government. They have no conception of what freedom and liberty mean.

2. We learn from the "Laws of Imitation" that any strong movement starts with a minority and then through imitation and contagion the majorty may follow. But the "leadership" must be such that a form of spiritual frenzy maintains the momentum.

Both of the above factors require time for education and development. New beliefs have to be established in the people's minds; beliefs that stir discontent and dissatisfaction with the prevailing system of society.

It would appear probable from a study of the characteristics of revolutions that any permanent change in the form of society in Russia will require long dreary years. At least it would appear prudent to be contrary to current hopes for an early total collapse of the Russian Soviet regime.

THEORY OF CONTRARY OPINION HINGES ON LAWS OF IMITATION AND CONTAGION

The writer wishes again to mention Gabriel Tarde's *The Laws of Imitation*. It is too bad this important book is so difficult to turn up in secondhand bookshops, but a few libraries have it, of course.

Professor Giddings' introduction to Tarde tells us that Tarde's philosophical theories and creativeness carne not only from keen observation but from ttmuch solitude and patient reflection." Most of us can't stand being alone more than half an hour, and our idea of reflection is merely to reflect and repeat what someone has told us! (We're imitators, that is.)

Described as a born student of human nature, Tarde was persistently interested in "the oldest of philosophical problems—the explanation of motive." He perceived not only that motive may be resolved into terms of belief and desire, but also that it can be measured.

Imitation is, indeed, a powerful motive (as Tarde demonstrates). Closely allied with it is "contagion," so comprehensively discussed by Gustave Le Bon in his several books,,

The Theory of Contrary Opinion hinges on these "laws" of imitation and contagion. It is therefore suggested that we keep these two "social ideas" constantly in mind, and occasionally to reflect on their potency as motivators of crowd behavior.

Tarde contends that there is no logical "separation" between the voluntary and involuntary, between the conscious and unconscious, imitation of ideas or acts. If one unconsciously and involuntarily reflects the opinions of others, or allows an action of others to be suggested to him, he imitates the idea or act—just the same as if he deliberately or knowingly borrowed the ideas or copied the acts.

Tarde also reminds us that "there are two ways of imitating, as a matter of fact; namely, to act exactly like one's model, or to do exactly the contrary. . . . Nothing can be affirmed without suggesting, no matter how simple the social environment, not only the idea that is affirmed, but the negative of this idea as well." How quickly come to mind the numerous social controversies of the present and the past twenty years, in this two-way respect. So we have to consider both imitating and *counter*imitating when considering our significant social and economic questions.

However, it is important to bring out that counterimitating arises from direct imitating in that "leadership" is present in the contrary action. As an example, a labor group may take an exactly contrary course to a trend in industry although the trend is being imitated by business generally. Yet, the "counterimitation" within labor circles is initiated by the leaders.

"Every positive affirmation," says Tarde, "at the same time that it attracts to itself mediocre and sheeplike minds,

arouses somewhere or other in a brain that is naturally re-
bellious—a negation that is diametrically opposite. . . ."

WHERE WILL MASS CONFORMITY LEAD?

Everything is becoming so "big" that one wonders if the
individual will get lost in the shuffle of vast undertakings
and technological mysteries.

> If people ("the crowd") become further
> emmeshed within what you might term "a pattern
> of uniform conformity," will (a) mass movements
> gain even greater intensity and increased cohesion
> and (b) will the individualist find it increasingly dif-
> ficult to hold his place in the enveloping "bigness"
> of socio-economic affairs?

This is a natural "think subject" for Libertarians. Our
Founding Fathers designed their scheme of government
not only on the idea of an independent and free nation, but
also on the revered notion of independent, liberty-loving,
and free-thinking *individuals*.

The fast early growth of this wonderful nation of ours
was due to the extraordinary accomplishments of individual
entrepreneurs. They were fast builders, these economic pioneers (sometimes scathingly called "buccaneers" by leftists
in our midst).

Indeed, they built so fast and furious that their second
step—of combining enterprises and pyramiding one on top
of another—has led to the submersion of individual effort
and the fostering of group effort and the conformity of individuals to a mass pattern. One of the questions which

may be asked today, when an employee of a huge corporate combine is being considered for advancement, is this: Is he a company man? Is he an individualist or does he conform to the company pattern? Does he subscribe to the gospel of "groupthink"? Bluntly, does he conform? Nothing, perhaps, is more frustrating to an individualist than to be mired in a modern group-led, massive, corporate organization. T'ne unfortunate guy should get out and seek contentment elsewhere, regardless of the loss of the security which goes with conformity. The "company" is better off because the huge outfits can no longer be operated for the benefit of individuals, and the man is better off because he'll never contribute his share to the company's progress. As the majority are happier when they conform, there will always be a supply of "company men." Nonconformists are in the tiny minority.

You cannot "blame" anyone for this development in American business. It has simply grown that way. Business organizations have become too large for individual management. We have entered the era of group management. Mass conformity has, naturally, gone along.

However, one of the connective problems, for us contrarians, is to ponder this thought: May it not be that cyclical movements will be of greater (rather than lesser) intensity in the future, because of this development of mass conformity?

THE THEORY OF CONTRARY OPINION
DEALS WITH DELUSIONS AND MASS
MISCONCEPTIONS

Let us discuss the theory of contrary opinion as it applies to certain socio-political delusions and misconceptions held by the masses.

There is, I believe, a significant and fallacious idea being inculcated in the public mind to which we contrarians need to pay critical attention.

I refer to the so-called "middle-road philosophy." Here is the gist of the fallacy: Middle-roaders can do harm to the Amencan way of economic life *because* they lead people to believe in socio-economic theories which can be put into practice *only by the methods and programs of left-wingers.*

This is basic reasoning, if you will think about it a moment. A middle-road philosophy preaches the better-things-of-life for ALL . . . *but* it also includes (or certainly implies) that if the economic system gets out of whack it is the duty of the State to step in and get the machinery back in smooth running order again.

Middle-roaders, therefore (perhaps unintentionally, I'm willing to concede), foster misconceptions and delusions concerning the functions of a "free" socio-economic system. What I am driving at is this: If you impress people (who have neither the time nor the inclination to study socio-political trends) that you believe the capitalistic cycles of business activity, production, employment, and prices, can be eliminated, or at least be "smoothed out" (a popular middle-road expression), you are, in my judgment, deluding the masses. There is no evidence in history which demonstrates that this has been accomplished, short of dictatorships or during periods of tight wartime controls.

> You cannot control or regulate the laws of demand and supply and at the same time retain the freedom of action which is the fundamental concept of the American system of private enterprise.

So it comes as something of a shock to observe comments forthcoming from prominent economists that they foresee the coming "breakup of the economic cycle"—and that our economic system is "on trial." Moreover, they apparently subscribe to middle-road philosophy that the government must be quick to intervene when something goes wrong.

This is where the theory of contrary thinking comes into its own. "Watch your idols" (popular ideas and terms). Doubt all propaganda before you believe it.

LOOKING TWO WAYS AT ONCE

One objective in the Theory of Contrary Opinion is to anticipate by being contrary. I use the word "anticipate" here in the dictionary sense of "consider or mention before the proper time." Please note there is an important distinction between "anticipate" and "predict." I look upon the theory of contrary opinion as an antidote to general predictions—through contrary anticipations—rather than as a method of definitive forecasting.

For example—and this is prompted by a helpful letter from the directing head of a well-known research bureau—you can anticipate either one of two (or more) trends or events—or you may anticipate *both*, awaiting further developments prior to settling upon which you think is the more probable.

Take, as a case in question, the economic outlook which has confronted us in recent years.

The "either/or" has been: Are we to have a renewed inflationary binge or a slump?

Note, however, that a contrary anticipation means "considering or mentioning before the proper time." That is a significant point in the Theory of Contrary Opinion.

In this connection I am asked, during a boom, this question: "Why, if you think the recovery, or boom, has further to go, do you start talking ahead of time about the slump to follow?" An excellent and pointed query.

The reply hinges upon two considerations: (1) The "time element," and (2) what we'll term the "psychological factor."

It has been my observation over a long period that it takes us average humans a considerable interval to shift our viewpoints, once we have established a given mental outlook. That is, if we have (mentally) accepted a trend as moving in one direction, we are not inclined to change our outlook *until well after the trend turns.* You have witnessed this phenomenon time and again, I know. However, if we adopt a contrary course and try to anticipate a change in the current, we're more likely to recognize the signs of an approaching whirlpool or precipitous drop than if we merely assume that if the river is smooth here it must be smooth all the way. It is difficult to cope with sudden changes, especially when unexpected. You've heard the Wall Street expression—"He stayed too bearish (or too bullish) too long."

The other consideration—the time element—we've discussed so often we need not refer to it again, except to reiterate that it is practically impossible to *time* economic trends and events accurately. Accordingly, the contrary theory makes no bones or apologies about being "early" in anticipations. We leave the pin-point guessing to others. Indeed, I might add that if you're not *early*, you'll probably be *late*.

THE TICKLISH BUSINESS OF FORECASTING

Business forecasting was never more difficult; yet businessmen have to look ahead if they are going to plan their policies advantageously.

The added difficulty today lies in the fact that the nation is neither in a peace economy nor in a war economy. Former yardsticks of postwar eras cannot measure the complicated status prevailing. It is complicated because:

1. Productive facilities have expanded to an extent which permits both the supplying of public and government (defense-war) demands.

   How to weigh the probabilities in this two-dimensional economy constitutes a real feat of guessability, because-

2. Government intervention in any number of economic factors—at unknown and unexpected times—completely alters the length of the measuring rod. Government rnay intervene in monetary and credit matters; in stockpiling of cotnmodities; in reduced or

expanded war orders; in actions or statements which affect sentiment; and in other ways. Such sudden shifts are unpredictable, obviously, as they depend upon world events, upon decisions arrived
at secretly in security sessions, or upon sudden developments
brought about by mass psychology.

Notwithstanding these complexities, economic predictions continue to be voluminous and persistent.
Likewise, they frequently continue to be something less
than accurate!

Because of the significant role played by government in
our modern economics, it becomes increasingly necessary
(in this writer's view) to pay particular attention to business
and public psychology.

One method for measuring this phase is the theory of contrary opinion, whereby the apparent majority viewpoint may be checked by analyzing the
"opposites."

Here's a little book which will hold you down to fundamentals in your business forecasting; yet you can absorb it
in a week (only 120 pages; includes 32 charts). It was published in early 1954 by the Journal of Commerce, as compiled by Dr. H. E. Luedicke, its brilliant editor. Title: *How
to Forecast Business Trends—A Special Report for Executives.* I
suggest you look into it. (I consider the *Journal of Commerce*
almost essential for anyone who follows and forecasts business trends.)

WHAT'S THE USE OF IT ALL?

From the heading you would get the idea that this contrary ruminator was about to jump off the bridge at midnight.

Quite the opposite is the case; he'd much rather dump a lot of useless knowledge into the creek.

This is the reaction I get whenever I spend hours browsing through the numerous old books and publications in my library out in the barn. I'm tempted each time to dump a lot of the stuff into the Saxtons River, feeling I would walk back refreshed. Then again it comes to me that one benefits, in a contrary manner, from the useless and fallacious information which gathers dust and cobwebs—but which, when written, was the "last word" on the subject. They'd best be retained as a reminder of the *wrong* words on the subjects.

So I keep it all to keep from believing that anyone has yet found the key to consistently accurate socio-economic forecasting.

> So long as human nature remains inconstant and changeable—and unpredictable—socio-economic trends will likewise remain unpredictable and subject to unexpected shifts.

Fundamentally, a common error we're all prone to fall into is mixing cause with effect.

As you browse over the opinions which have been published through the years—in eras of good times and bad—you are struck over and over again by how often the *prevailing* conditions produced the opinions; how what was happening at the time was looked upon as the cause of events continuing to happen in the same pattern. Little effort was made to analyze what had happened previously— things which would *cause a change in the future.*

We are unconsciously influenced by what is *now* taking place. If a boom exists, the bullish and optimistic arguments are the most popular and "acceptable." If a slump prevails, pessimism and discouragement are contagious.

Government intervention in a given socio-economic situation (monetarily, as in the present era, for example) is caused *by* (the result of) a prior condition or maladjustment. Yet it is often looked upon merely as a current event, the reason for the interference being overlooked or disregarded.

Perhaps I may assert that a primary value in the theory of contrary opinion is that it forces one to probe behind the surface effects in order to get at the causes. Moreover, it is a constant reminder that *the present is a forerunner of change in the near future.*

MAYBE SOME OLD THEORIES ARE STILL VALID

My bedside reading table usually holds an odd assortment of books. One which remained beside me for several weeks was Emerson's volume of essays, *The Conduct of Life.*

Being what my liberal friends term 'tan old fogy," I derive considerable pleasure and stimulation from older books, while still enjoying new ones. I confess to being a realistic reactionary, one who would like to return to some of the older, sounder, preNew-Deal socio-political theories, but one who realizes we won't!

Perhaps you'll like to refresh your recollection of Emerson's essay on 'Wealth." Asserting that "Wealth brings with it its own checks and balances," Emerson, a wise American, adds these remarks:

. . . The basis of political economy is [should be] noninterference. The only safe rule is found in the self-adjusting meter of demand and supply. Do not legislate. Meddle, and you snap the sinews with your sumptuary laws. Give no bounties, make equal laws, secure life and property, and you need not give alms. Open the doors of opportunity to talent and virtue and they will do themselves justice, and property will not be in bad hands. In a free and just commonwealth, property rushes from the idle and imbecile to the industrious, brave and persevering.

The laws of nature play through trade. . . . The level of the sea is not more surely kept than is the equilibrium of value in society by the demand and supply; and artifice or legislation punishes itself by reactions, gluts and bankruptcies. . . .

Space limits quotations—but perhaps you'll dig out your old volume of Ralph Waldo's essays and become reacquainted. He wasn't such an old fogy at that!

Books have a habit of sending you on fascinating haunts: Emerson, in the above, to old and new economic tomes to see the veerings of ideas and thoughts.

"NEUTRALISM"—IN ECONOMIC WRITING

It has become quite the fashion to add an "ism" to words these days. So I'll adopt the habit in the heading above.

Not long ago a prospective subscriber to our *Letters of Contrary Opinion* wrote us a very courteous note. After reading two or three sample *Letters*, he said he found them "rather interesting; however to me they sound neutral. . . .'"

He then added: "I like something more definite; so for the above reason I cannot subscribe to your Letters at this time."

I am using this for a note on the theory of contrary opinion, because I think it brings out a significant point to ruminate over in connection with economic writings. It is a simple matter to be dogmatic and definite when one is writing on a given economic subject or trend. A commentator can pick up a collection of comments from economists and analysts, jot down the composite conclusions expressed, and then write out a blunt "opinion."

However, there is a serious drawback to being dogmatic in economic comments. Rather, there are *two* drawbacks to be considered:

a) More often than not, a given economic trend may be *unpredictable at the time of writing about it.* Therefore, a definite or dogmatic statement is merely a guess expressed as if it were knowledge.

b) Moreover, when definite statements become *generalized* they are likely to "defeat themselves."

It is common to bemoan the confused state of affairs, when we're trying to arrive at decisions. Quite often, however, we use the confusion as an excuse for not thinking.

I, contrarily, believe there is value in bewilderment.

Consider the opposite of uncertainty and confusion; namely, *dogmatism.* I dare to say that more important errors in decisions arise from dogmatic opinions than from what I shall call "confused considerations."

If, when you're confused and uncertain, you put the matter in the back of your mind and let it sort of kaleidoscope around until the various pieces of the problem take on definite shape and meaning, you will find the uncertainty fading away.

The result is that, from initial bewilderment over a given problem, you come up with a thoroughly thought-out solution.

This writer—whose task it is to examine *contrary* viewpoints—looks upon his writing duties in this light: to measure as accurately as possible the composite *definite* commentaries on prevailing trends . . . that is step one . . . then to ruminate over the opposite possibilities and probabilities and pass them on as *ruminations*, not as dogmatic opinions. (After all, one man's opinions are no more likely to be correct than those of any economic observer. *But* a breakdown of other observers' opinions, and how those opinions may prove wrong, is often of value.)

I like to think of contrary thinking as "thought starters." Visualize, if you will, a management committee sitting around a table discussing forward trends and policies. Suppose a contrary fellow every now and then breaks in and asks: "Have you thought about the matter from this angle?" Or—"Suppose, gentlemen, that those forecasts yot're reading happen to be wrong: what then will be your policy?" Such contrary checking can be valuable.

One doesn't go into committee meetings and blurt out *unsupported assertions*. If you do, you're not invited back to the next meeting! On the other hand, it is frequently impossible (if you're truthful) to support contrary viewpoints with definite conclusions. Contrary opinions are "thoughts before leaping" to prevent "jumps before concluding."

BE A NONCONFORMIST IN YOUR THINKING

Mass psychology is an absorbing study. Let us consider the extremes of general public optimism and pessimism. You'll observe a peculiar twist of human nature. When economic affairs are booming and "everybody" feels cheerful, optimistic, and prosperous, no one wants to hear disparaging remarks or bad news about how things are going. People wish to enjoy their optimism. They do *not* wish a wet blanket thrown over their wishful thinking. If someone suggests that booms and periods of optimism always overshoot the mark and bring about corrective reactions, the said someone is called a "prophet of gloom." He is politely (or impolitely) told to shut his pessimistic mouth.

That is one side of the coin of human traits.

At another time, when the economy has been slumping and "times are bad," then the opposite psychology prevails. People then wish to enjoy their misery. They do not wish that wet blanket removed. They get into the frame of mind that allows them to believe that everything is in bad shape. What is more, they expect things will remain that way.

It seems to be a fixed trait of human nature that people (as a mass) get their minds into a rut in accordance with the ruling trends.

Rut-thinking is a common trait. I have said that the art of contrary thinking may be stated simply: Thrust your thoughts out of a rut. Be a nonconformist when using your mind.

A worth-while side light on this idea of being a nonconformist in the use of your mind might be mentioned: You are thereby more contented in your everyday life, and more relaxed in your thinking. You are not frustrated or taken by surprise when events happen and when trends turn. You're ready for what comes.

The nonconformist knows that life is full of ups and downs. When everything is *up* he recognizes that there will be a time ahead when everything will be down.

Being a nonconformist, he further recognizes that the ups and downs are not predictable as to extent or duration. He therefore cares little for precise "tops" or "bottoms"— he doesn't try to measure the exact magnitude of the ups and downs because he knows there is no reliable yardstick.

If you wish to bring this philosophy down to its practical application you will be comfortably cogitating on what your plans will be when the *up* shifts to *down* . . . and vice versa.

MORE ON SOCIO-POLITICAL TRENDS

This contrarian, as you know, lays great stress on the socio-economic trends. These trends are not stationary. Political, social, and economic trends evolve—and revolve. History reveals both a steady growth factor and cyclical characteristics in sociopolitico-economic trends.

The reason the contrarian needs to be aware of history, in this regard, is because changes in trend occur before the masses are *consciously observant* of the fact. Al- so, because when socio-political conditions seem to revolve and repeat, the average person (of brief memory) is unaware of the "cycle" and is likely to think that a "new" condition has developed.

By way of illustration, let me quote something: "Whither is France tending; whither Europe? This is the question which is exercising the minds of all at the present moment and to which an answer has yet to be vouchsafed." This certainly reflects a problem of today—yet it was written over thirty years ago. The writer went on to say:

Has not the time arrived for our political leaders to think of taking their bearings? Very able craftsmen as most of them are, they unfurl their sail and direct the rudder to perfection, according as the wind veers at this game, they are led by chance and the harbor is never in sight. Were they to search outside the superficial contingencies of the hour, into the remote spaces and vistas of the past, they would find the "co-ordinates" which would enable them to fix their course. But a careful study of history is little thought of in these days of rapid change, of living from hand to mouth. Grave indeed is the situation, when even governments, whose essential role is to foresee, refuse to look ahead; when unstable democracies, in their political capacity, are satisfied with little more than the prospect of the next elections.

A rather lengthy quote, but much to think about! This appears in a worth-while book, written in 1924- 25, and published in 1927 by the Viking Press, *Political Myths and Economic Realities*, by Francis

Delaisi. I've used it to bring out the thought that *today's* trends are affected by those of the past, and that earlier problems—if unsolved—may return in magnified forms to plague the world and its statesmen.

The author of the above book asserts that the growth of human societies depends upon "three ele-

mental forces: *permanent needs, variable institutions* (by which these needs are satisfied), and the *ideas* entertained by the masses of these institutions and ideas." These three elements are constantly in motion; they constitute what he terms "a force of movement" which sometimes is at odds with "the force of inertia" *(as people oppose change)*. At other times, the force of movement may run along with public sentiment.

Basically, people desire *stability and security*. But in seeking this social "constant" they may succumb to socio-political "myths" and delusions that lead to instability and insecurity. There is then the return road which has to be traversed.

THINKING HUMANISTICALLY AS WELL AS REALISTICALLY

I'm quite taken, as I think you'd be, with a little book published in 1950 titled *Economic Ideas; A Study of Historical Perspectives,* by Ferdynand Zweig (Prentice-Hall, Inc.).

Zweig's viewpoints are largely from a European angle, he having been at one time Professor of Political Economy at the University of Cracow, and more recently at the University of Manchester. However, a European viewpoint is rather to be de-. sired, I think, in ruminating over historical trends and perspectives, because shifts in ideas and trends have been made earlier abroad than here and also, of course, because we have no long-time history of economic philosophies.

You might claim with some justification that Adam Smith fathered the economic philosophy which guided our capitalistic system up to the time of the New Deal and the Keynesian doctrine (which sprang from Lord Keynes' influential writings and his major tome, *General Theory of Employment, Interest and Money*). One of Zweig's more entertaining sections is his comparison of Keynes' and John Law's theories of money.

It is perspectively interesting to note that Adam Smith published his famous *Wealth of Nations* in the same year that Jefferson wrote our great Declaration of Independence.

You did not see much veering toward "neosocialism" in America until after the Great Depression; whereas the leftward drift had set in in Europe and England well over a half century earlier (see Herbert Spencer's penetrating *The Man Versus the State,* reprinted by The Caxton Printers, Ltd., with a Foreword by Albert J. Nock). As Nock remarks, Spencer describes "how in the latter half of the last century British Liberalism went over bodily to the philosophy of Statism."

There are some observers today who profess to foresee a swing back toward conservatism, all over the world (including here in the United States) , but this contrarian does not share their optimism. I venture to think that our formerly conservative political party, the Republican, will be even more "liberal" in its appeals to voters in 1956. (This is being written prior to the 1956 Presidential "Messages" and campaign pronouncements.)

I have run away from my title, above. I started to emphasize a comment of Zweig's, where he complained that economic writers "have excluded their hearts from the study
of man . . ." adding that "economics after all is and will remain the study of man, and a study of man of vital importance, of great possibilities, and with a great future before
it. No study of man can succeed unless the heart has a part
in it."

As this writer visualizes the usefulness of the theory of
contrary opinion, it is, as you know, the human approach,
not merely the figures, which must at all times be considered. Thinking humanistically as well as realistically is essential.

THINKING IN CIRCLES

When you analyze "opinions," to learn how they germi-
nate, you find they commonly sprout from influences outside the mind. Seeds of (cursory) thought are planted by
some happening, or propaganda, from which they often
blossom into colorful opinions. Thus it is that mass opinions tend to follow, rather than to lead, "events." Frequently,
be- cause of the emotions aroused, you note changing conditions and socio-economic developments evolving into
generalized opinions.

Cursory thinking may be likened to the paring of
an apple: it does not reach the core, but merely
slices off the surface of "what everybody thinks."
Thinking in circles seldom gets anywhere—except

to follow the mode of the moment and the opinion of the hour.

For instance, boom conditions create highly hopeful and optimistic "thoughts." Depressed conditions cause depressed sentiments and pessimism.

During prosperous periods human traits in the ascendency are greed, hope, susceptibility, impulsiveness, pride-of-opinion, and wishful thinking. Let us add credulity, for people are credulous in booms.

When slumps occur, other traits take over people's thinking, such as fear, irritability, indecisivenessand incredulity and doubt.

Two motivating opinion makers—Imitation and Contagion—are "constants," however. They remain in action throughout the revolutions.

If this writer were asked how to keep from thinking in circles, he would reply (obviously) : "Adopt the contrary approach; first reverse the circle, then bore in for deeper soundings." Professor Robert P. Crawford would tell you to "Own your own mind and learn to challenge things." (*Think. For Yourself* is the title of an excellent book by Professor Crawford —not now in print, I believe.)

These manifestations of follow-the-leader thinking are witnessed in all phases of our daily living— in politics, in social affairs, in fashions, in business decisions, in games of chance, and markets.

In economic dealings you might put it this way:

The "crowd" is most enthusiastic and optimistic when it should be cautious and prudent; and is most fearful when it should be bold.

"... STILL DOESN'T KNOW WHAT MAKES HIM TICK"

Some years back we wrote one of our pieces on the negative idea of faulty forecasting. In so doing, we were replying to queries about the Theory of Contrary Opinion . . . queries such as we still receive: When to be contrary? What intensity of overall opinions to look for when "going contrary"? How to measure general opinions? And so on. . . .

I mentioned then, and repeat now, that we need not be too discouraged if we do not always grasp contrary viewpoints, because the whole field of economics remains a "guessy" one. Little, if any, progress has been made over the years in attaining profitable accuracy in economic (or in market) forecasting.

It was and is my contention that "crowd psychology" is the missing tool that will help you to jimmy the window so you may get a look at varying future viewpoints.

I have dared to assert time and again that you may have all the statistics in the world at your finger tips, but still you do not know how or why people are going to act.

So it was that you may imagine my interest when I picked up the Sunday paper and read that "a top psychologist took a look at the American consumer and acknowledged that he still doesn't know what makes him tick."

"Man as a consumer," said Professor James J. Gibson, of Cornell, "still eludes the theories of present-day psychology. And the dullest customer can still laugh up his sleeve at the smartest psychologist who pretends to control his buying behavior."

The problem is partially solved when you recall that *Contagion* and *imitation* are *twin motives*. They influence "buying behaviors" more than is generally realized.

It is not solely a matter of the pocketbook, but of the mind and the emotions.

The Theory of Contrary Opinion won't give you second sight or the power of prophecy. You can, however, analyze "going opinions" and consider how they may "go opposite." Influenced by contagion, imitation, and traits which are always present—such as greed, hope, fear, pride-of-opinion, envy, and impulsiveness—opinions often do an about-face, as we know. People who had no intention of buying, suddenly splurge. (Haven't you experienced similar reactions yourself?)

When everybody thinks alike, everyone is likely to be wrong, to repeat the slogan of the Contrary Theory. Anyway, our theory undertakes to deal with the fact that no one knows what makes the American consumer tick, by going at it in reverse.

THREE TYPES OF "OPINIONS" — THOUGHTFUL, THOUGHTLESS, EMOTIONAL

In considering the uses and interpretations of the Theory of Contrary Opinion, it is essential to determine under what circumstances the popular views originate.

Opinions vary in accordance with the degree of thought or emotion involved. An off-hand reply to a question may be directly opposite to an opinion that might arise in an emotionally excited group, or crowd. A thoughtful opinion may be quite different from either of the others.

An example of the off-hand type was noted on an interview program I listened to recently. German students were being asked various questions about living in West Berlin, how they felt about the eastern zone, and so on. The interviewer then put a pointed question to the group: "Would you fight to protect West Berlin from the Communists?" The reply of three or four of the group was unhesitating: "No," they said in substance, "we wouldn't go to war over Berlin."

This subjective reply—and an off-hand one—merely reflected their feelings, fears and hatred of war; emotions that have been built up in their consciousnesses since the devastation of World War II, and from their hatred of Red Russia.

A war spirit is an aroused emotion. That is the distinction in this particular illustration. A government doesn't go around quietly asking people if they wish to go to war. A series of charges against the "enemy state" is trumped up; cries against the aggressor pour forth, as the propaganda machine gets in motion. An image is fashioned in the peoples' minds of this dangerous, armed "imperialist" who is about to take their homes and ruin their existence.

In other words, foul propaganda is employed to stir up hatred against the "enemy" (who before may have been a friendly trading partner in world goods) . When the emotions are kindled to a high heat the masses will actually want war, and the government can take the position that war was forced upon it, the people demanded it.

Not much is needed for a discussion of the "thoughtful opinion" but I'm confident you are aware of how different a well-thought-out opinion is from one that is caught on the fly, so to speak, or one that is merely a reflection of a crowd's fears or hopes. An individual may think out his opinions, whereas a crowd is swayed by emotional viewpoints rather than by reasoning or reason-why arguments.

Emotional and thoughtless opinions spread widely from imitation and contagion.

HOW OPINIONS ARE FORMED

Have you ever considered how opinions are formed? Obviously, a few million people do not sit down of a Sunday morning and suddenly arrive at an opinion.

Opinions are planted in people's minds and sprout when fertilized.

I was ruminating over this not long ago when a story in the *New York Times* caught my attention. It was a report from London, just prior to Prime Minister Macmillan's trip to Moscow. In a speech, the Prime Minister stressed no appeasement. Here is how Drew Middleton, well-known Times' correspondent, described it:

> Mr. Macmillan's references to appeasement and retreat in a speech to a national rally of young Conservatives were intended to answer critics in the United States and in Western Europe and to instruct public opinion in Britain, sources close to him disclosed....

The italics are mine. The report supports the assertion that opinions are put in people's minds. Not often is so telling a comment found in the public print.

None of us can estimate the vast amount of *opinion-forming* that is attempted in our reading matter. Newspapers and magazines (and privately printed "letters") are loaded with viewpoints and impressions—some true-to-facts, a lot of it misleading, and a good deal of it misinformed or false. Propagandists of all stripes run their mimeograph machines night and day to create ideas and opinions in our minds. One editor in a large news-syndicating office told me that 90 per cent of the news we read is "manufactured" by publicists, public-relations experts, and by specialists in influencing the Mind of the Crowd. The figure is no doubt exaggerated, but the condition exists to a far greater degree than readers realize.

When speaking of manufactured news, don't overlook the government agencies. Opinion-building is constantly at work in Washington, London, Paris, and in Moscow.

As Dr. Abram Lipsky explains in his excellent book with long title, Man The Puppet: The Art of Controlling Minds; Persuasion is Part of the Art of Government: "It is the business of leaders and statesmen to FORM public opinion, to direct the thought of a nation in predetermined ways."

Confirming my remarks above, Dr. Lipsky says "the so-called opinions that one hears in conversations are well-known to be duplicates sent out by makers of opinion." He further states that on public matters few men have opinions"—to which we might add that the same holds true in economics and finance. Most people take their financial-economic opinions, as they do their stock-market viewpoints, from tips, overheard conversations, columns and advertisements, and from gossip about what the mythical "they" are doing or are going to do.

Thus are opinions formed and spread. Contagion works fast. Moreover, inasmuch as crowd-opinions are seldom well-founded, and frequently ill-timed, it is found that CONTRARY opinons are indispensable to clear and accurate thinking.

READ-AND-NEEDLE IS THE CONTRARY WAY

There is tight and loose thinking, just as there is tight and loose money. And you can say there is a mental gap as well as a dollar gap.

I'm convinced, however, that the application of serious contrary thinking and ruminating go a long way toward correcting thinking deficiencies. It takes mental discipline to practice contrary thinking—to read and needle—but those of us who have made the effort feel well repaid, I'm sure.

There is a vast difference, as I see it, between an open mind and a gapping mind. An active open mind is ready for ideas—pro and con—and is prepared to arrive at a conclusion. An open mind is not a wishy-washy one, whereas a gapping thoughtapparatus takes in opinions and ideas of others and goes to sleep on them without further examination.

Occasionally I'm told that my contrary comments in my *Letters* are not definite enough.

This brings up a point we have discussed which bears repeating. Forcing oneself to be definite and specific can cause more wrong guesses and forecasts than anything I can think of. It has given rise to the cynical expression: "Often in error, but never in doubt."

It is this writer's contention, after over 30 years' acquaintance with, and observation of, economics and Wall Street that being POSITIVE, SPECIFIC, and DOGMATIC is about the most harmful habit one can fall into.

If you are positive, or dogmatic, about a given subject or event you obviously cannot ruminate over it contrarily. Isn't that true? Think it over.

The value of the contrary approach is the opposite. It prevents one from being a dogmatist; one avoids being *positive about conjectural* matters; as one reads, he mentally needles the writer or commentator; finally, he is forced to make up his own mind instead'of accepting the opinions of others (which likely as not are fallacious).

I am confident that the chief reason the "investment advisory business" has had a poor record over the years is that writers of advisory bulletins feel compelled by *client demands* to be specific, dogmatic, and bold—*at all times.* Turn to the October, 1959, issue of *Fortune* if you're interested in checking this assertion. Read the article, "Stock-Market Letters: A Growth Situation." The magazine takes it upon itself to criticize letters-that-have-gone-wrong, doubtless overlooking the thought that Fortune, too, has suffered from wrong guesses. The fault lies (1) in the pernicious desire of writers in the financialeconomic field to FORECAST—to be oracles. Once bitten, it is difficult to effect a cure! Readers (2) are equally at fault in expecting that anyone can predict economic or market trends accurately and consistently.

THE THEORY OF CONTRARY OPINION AND THE "TRIADIC LAW"

I'll probably gct in over my head, but I should like to try to bring out a logical basis for our Theory of Contrary Opinion.

Inasmuch as contrary thinking falls into three parts, it may be said to follow the triadic law of Logic. However, you might term it "the synthetical" as opposed to "the syllogistic" method.

Let us turn to the philosophers rather than the logicians for our "formula."

The German, Johann Gottlieb Fichte (1762-1814) , is credited, I believe, with formulating the triad of thesis, antithesis, and synthesis — but it was Hegel who developed it into a philosophical system of "perpetual thought." Let me give you an interpretation from the *Encyclopaedia Britannica* (Hegel — 11th edition) : "Every truth, every reality, has three aspects or stages; it is the unification of two contradictory elements, of two partial aspects of truth which are not merely contrary, like black and white, but contradictory, like same and different. The first step is a preliminary affirmation and unification, the second a negation and differentiation, the third a final synthesis."

Applying the formula of thesis, antithesis, and synthesis to the theory of contrary opinion, you may establish the three stages something like this:

A. The general opinion (prevailing thesis).
B The contrary, or skeptical analysis (the antithesis).
C. The conclusion you arrive at (or synthesis of the common and opposing viewpoints).

The more I learn about the *use* of contrary thinking, the more I come to the conclusion that I have not always given enough weight to the idea of *synthesis*.

Here's what I mean: Instead of leaping abruptly from affirmation to its opposite (from general opinions to contrary opinions) , we need to consider the synthesis (combination) of *parts* of general opinions and their opposites. That is, not every element of a generalized opinion may be wrong, or ill-timed, but only certain phases, or aspects, of the generallyheld viewpoint.

I suppose our process of thought should be something on this order: Take the leap from the General Opinion to its Opposite (or from affirmation to negation) and then, from the ideas thus released, work back to a speculative and reflective conclusion, or synthesis. In this way, we may avoid denying *facts* which are elements in the generalized opinions we are analyzing contrarily.

As *an aside*, does it not appear that over the long future, the synthesis of communism and capitalism (opposites), will be "a little of each"? Shall we not continue to veer toward a socialized capitalism while the communists drift into a form of capitalistic socialism?

"SOCIAL PRESSURE OFTEN BREEDS CONFORMITY"

In an issue of the *Industrial Bulletin*, published by the noted research organization of Arthur D. Little, Inc., some recent experiments were referred to. An article in the *Bulletin* commented that "social pressure often breeds conformity; the individual's decisions are influenced by what has been called, at different times and by different people, environment, group pressure, or propaganda."

Perhaps some of you saw a report in the *Scientific American* by Dr. Solomon E. Asch, which described the experiments mentioned.

What Dr. Asch attempted was a measurement of the degree to which contrary group opinion can cause an individual to amend his personal judgment. "Put more succinctly, the experiments studied the 'engineering of consent' " (which, by the way, is the title of a recent book, edited by Edward Bernays in which our theoty of contrary opinion is used to illustrate "the strategy of reversal").

The experiments: (To quote) Seven to nine young men compared, by eye, the lengths of vertical black lines on two large white cards. One bore a standard line; the other had three lines, of which one was identical to the standard.

In initial comparisons, there was agreement. Then, one man (the subject of the experiment) found himself disagreeing with his colleagues who by prearrangement had been instructed to give wrong answers. Further line-matching measured the subject's ability to resist the pressure of the opinion *of the group.*

Weighing the "evidence of his senses" against the opinion of the group, the subject had to state his opinion publicly, in the face of majority opinion to the contrary. The position of the majority was frequently (and purposely) the wrong one; out of 18 trials in each series of experiments, the majority gave 12 wrong answers.

To summarize briefly, the average individual tested lost his self-confidence. Whereas he would normally err less than one per cent, he swung to the position of the majority, and voted wrong 36.8 per cent of the time under group pressure. There was considerable spread, however, the report states, "about onequarter of the subjects tested never lost their independence of judgment, while conversely, some were never able to break free from the herd."

This was an interesting experiment in "conformity" and tends to confirm the usefulness of the theory of contrary opinion, as we learn more about how to use it.

MOMENTUM

The subject of MOMENTUM makes an acceptable essay—and might start up some chains of ideas in your mind.

Many of you doubtless think of momentum in its mechanical definition, which the dictionary would phrase something like this: A force of motion acquired by a moving body, being always proportioned to the mass multiplied into the velocity; momentum indicates the force or power that a

moving body exerts to maintain its motion. A falling body gains momentum.

We're going to get hopelessly involved, I'm afraid, if
we get over too far into engineering when what we're
concerned with in economics is the momentum which
is impelled, or retarded, by psychological influences.
There is a rule in psychology called 'Weber's Law,
which Walter Pitkin sagely defined as "Psychology's Law
of Diminishing Return." Briefly it means this:

> a.—to increase the intensity (momentum) of a
> *stimulus* in arithmetical progress, the stimulus
> must be increased in geometrical progress, so
> to speak.
> b.— to sustain the momentum (intensity) the
> stimulus must be constantly increased.

Moreover, "stimuli" may *react*: may bore, tire, irritate, become unfashionable, lose potency, et cetera. Momentum
thereupon is retarded, as intensity falls.

If you are satisfied that what people do with their money
and credit is the major motivating force in economics (motive: thought or feeling that makes one act) . . . as I say, if
you're satisfied with this motivating force, then surely we
can consider "momentum" in various economic series as a
condition that must constantly be observed. For instance,
the money managers attempt to control the momentum of
the use of credit and supply of money in order to curb and
curtail the wide fluctuations in the socalled business cycle.
(The momentum in the use of bank deposits is commonly

referred to as "turnover" whereas merchandise turnover—
ratio of sales to inventory—is termed "momentum of
sales." Wherever you turn in economics you run into "momentum," do you not? Economics is not static; it is a *moving*
"system.")

Carl Snyder, long brilliantly identified with the New York
Federal Reserve Bank, refers plainly in his splendid book
Capitalism The Creator to "the factors of momentum and inertia in economics." He addressed the American Association for the Advancement of Science on the subject of
"The Concept of Momentum and Inertia in Economics."
There are "mechanisms" constantly at work, as Snyder
shows, "in problems involving money and prices, profits
and progress, and in numerous other controversial questions. . . ." *The momentum of growth in America* is a precious
heritage, seldom interrupted.

MORE ON THE CONTRARY APPROACH TO CREATIVE THINKING

Not so long ago I received a letter from a Mr. Zuce
Kogan, of Chicago, who had the interest and boldness to
establish the Creative Thinking Institute a few years ago.
The Institute is dedicated primarily to problem solving for
industry, and has published a number of monographs and
books by Mr. Kogan.

In his letter to me Mr. Kogan makes an assertion which
is of interest to all Contrarians. He wrote about a recheck
they had been conducting concerning their "approaches."
(They use the word *approach* to refer to their methods of
problem solvirxg.)

When re-analyzing the approaches already enumerated (in our methods) I found that they were all based on the "opposite" or "contrary."
. . . It may sound peculiar that contrary thinking is required to achieve creative thoughts and is inherent in practically all of the approaches developed so far. This, however, becomes self-evident when we realize that thinking the way someone else thinks results in mimicry—a "copycat" requires the minimum of creative thought.

It is good news, of course, when others stress the values which we have long felt were inherent to the Theory of Contrary Opinion (as I have attempted to develop it over the years) . So let me give you a bit more of Mr. Kogan's thesis:

Therefore (in further reference to creative thinking), the inference is that to achieve any creativeness, some change has to be made. From this, it stands to reason that the optimum in creativeness must approach the maximum change . . . and the maximum change must be close to the opposite.

The ruminating which Mr. Kogan reflected as he dictated went a step further:

One may ask why develop "approaches" when all we want is to make a change, or in an extreme sense use the opposite. The answer is that knowing we have to make a change is not enough. We must know how to make the change, or how to apply the opposite. The approaches help to bring out the opposite or contrary inherent in the suggested solution. They circumscribe the situation at hand. In other words, "approaches" break up creative thinking into more digestible morsels.

MOTIVES AND MOVEMENTS

MOTIVE, as we learn from studies of crowd psychology and from Tarde's *Laws of Imitation,* "is the oldest of philosophical problems." Motive springs from "belief" and "desire" and "fear" (and similar traits) . Through imitation and contagion it may spread rapidly: from individuals to groups to nations.

Today you read as if it were something new about group studies that emphasize "motive research" (studies which spread over into "consumer preferences" and numerous business and advertising analytical problems) . Yet, the "discovery" will be found to have been discussed by economic philosophers of an earlier age, including Bentham, Cournot, Menger, Walras, Jevons, and particularly by Gabriel Tarde.

Similar problems confront us in our Theory of Contrary Opinion. Tarde claimed that motives could be measured, but in the rise and fall of "opinions" (arising from motives), I find the *measurement* of the *degree* of opinions at best a speculative estimate, or guess. Obviously, however, quantitative estimates are essential.

The degree to which a given opinion is accepted—how widespread and general it is—is significant when it comes to stressing or considering the *opposite* viewpoint, or condition (even if it must be conjectural).

One finds that over- and underestimates of the *generality* of crowd opinions on a given subject are not uncommon.

Notwithstanding such shortcomings, anyone who has examined even a few of the extraordinary forecasts and opinions which have gone wrong over the years (in war and peace, in finance and politics) will agree, I'm sure, that contrary considerations are useful in thinking and contribute to the gaining of wisdom.

PROTECT YOURSELF AGAINST THE "DEPTH MANIPULATORS"

We mention above how Gabriel Tarde dug deeply to learn about *motives*, and mentioned the modern trend toward research in this field. It is this current trend I should like to discuss with you for a moment.

Propaganda is a pointed factor in analyzing "opinions" because it is evident, I think, that propaganda, skillfully engineered, MANIPULATES OPINIONS. Elsewhere we have referred to various studies such as one titled "Groupthink" by Fortune magazine, comments on "conformity" and the "company man" —and referred to the book *Engineering of Consent*.

> We are now witnessing, and shall increasingly experience, "thought and desire manipulation" which is almost frightening to contemplate. I do not hesitate to assert that contrarianism offers protection against the Depth Manipulators . . . and I intend to make this especially pertinent.

Let me introduce you to the modern science of arousing our "hidden" desires that has brought into common usage the word "depth" — bandied about among practitioners of the art of Motivation Research, called M.R. for short. In their efforts to get us to buy what they have to offer (whether it may be products, beliefs, opinions, or votes), public relations and advertising experts actually do delve "beneath our level of awareness" (hit us when we ain't looking) . Call them Hidden Persuaders, which is the title a most interesting writer selected for his important book.

> *The Hidden Persuaders*, by Vance Packard, tells all. I urge you to read it. Here is what Mr. Packard says is a composite view of *you and me* as held by these depth manipulators: "Typically they see us as bundles of day dreams, misty hidden yearnings, guilt complexes, irrational emotional blockages. We are image lovers given to impulsive and compulsive acts. We annoy them with our seemingly senseless quirks, but we please them with our growing docility in responding to their manipulation of symbols that stir us to action. . . ." Briefly defined, "motivation research (M.R.) is the type of research that seeks to learn what motivates peoples in making choices," in the words of a Chicago practitioner.

When you know that our biggest advertisers have turned to this science of M.R. you must agree that, as Packard says, "these depth manipulators are . . . starting to acquire a power of persuasion" that warrants our attention. The book confirms the advisability of developing the "contrary approach" in our thinking, reading, and doing. Be sure to read it. (You are shown, for instance, how bullish propaganda is *planned to maintain an ever-confident public opinion.* A "little inflation" sounds so pleasant!)

MASS MESMERISM

It may appear an exaggeration to say that such a condition as mass mesmerism can exist. However, there have been many times in history when the "crowd" has indeed seemingly been hypnotized.

If you think of mesmerism or hypnosis as actually putting people to sleep physically, while their subconscious minds react to suggestions and commands of the hypnotist, then crowds are, of course, not mesmerized. However, a crowd hysteria can be, and has often been, created by the actions and harangues of a demagogue. The manner in which a mass of people will respond to such leadership is certainly similar to actual mesmerism.

LeBon, the long-accepted authority on crowd activities, writes that the leader has often started out as one of the led, explaining that:

> He (the leader) has been hypnotized by the idea whose apostle he has since become. It has taken possession of him to such a degree that everything outside vanishes, and that every contrary opinion appears to him an error or a superstition. An example in point is Robespierre, hypnotized by the philosophical ideas of Rousseau, and employing the methods of the Inquisition to propagate them.

In more recent history, no more glaring example is needed than to refer to Hitler. The former paper hanger had the masses under control for years. It seems unbelievable as you look back, but how realistic it all was while Hitler was in the ascendancy and held sway as an incredible "hypnotist." Hitler fitted the qualifications LeBon lays down for successful mob leaders: "They are especially recruited from the ranks of those morbidly nervous, excitable, half-deranged persons who are bordering on madness. However absurd may be the idea they uphold or the goal they pursue, their convictions are so strong that all reasoning is lost upon them. . . ."

To a far lesser extent than in those instances in history of vast mass movements and revolutions, we see crowd hypnotism at work in various directions.

The slavery to fashion changes comes under the head of mass mesmerism, I think. Otherwise, why would millions of people practically overnight, accept a given style fad? Take the youngsters who scream at the Presleys. The girls are uniformly dressed, as a rule, and the boys, too. You might term style changes more a case of imitation and contagion, perhaps, but the masses are mesmerized, in a sense.

There are economic beliefs (and illusions) which have become *accepted* through a form of mass mesmerism. A crowd is led to believe—to accept ideas —through *affirmation and repetition.* Tell 'em again and again, without explanation or proof, and in time the crowd will believe what you tell 'em. This is the way various liberal ideas and false notions of economic stability have finally become almost universally "taken for granted." Shall we be mesmerized to believe in the millenium?

... AGAIN ON THE QUESTION: "IS THE PUBLIC ALWAYS WRONG IN THE MARKET?"

This question comes up repeatedly during any discussion of the contrary theory. It is natural that it should come up, because the idea of money-making the easy way is a popular pastime. And of course it's a fallacy!

Perhaps no undertaking is more difficult than playing the stock market. Only a tiny fraction of those who attempt this "easy way to riches" ever succeed. What defeats them is a little matter of inherent characteristics. (1) A few persons are endowed with the money-making attribute (this, to my mind, you're born with; and if you haven't got it, you'd better forget it! I believe people either have a "money mind" or they haven't.) ; (2) Additionally, various human traits stand in the way of this pleasant method of getting rich without working for it, such as the emotional drawbacks of fear, hope, greed, wishfulthinking, and so on.

From these references you can see why the public is wrong so frequently in the stock market. However, a fairly correct, generalized reply to the question in the heading above might be expressed this way:

The "crowd" has always been found to be wrong when it counted most to be right. This is a bit quippish; a more sedate reply would be that the crowd is wrong at the *terminals* of trends, but is right, on the average, *during* the trends.

You find the public aiding and "pushing" the trends (up and down) —more actively when the stock market is going up than when it is in a prolonged bear trend. The public loses heart quickly when prices continue to slide off. Thus, we find public selling often increasing as the slide deepens; until finally, near the bottom "when all hope is lost" people dump their stocks—at a time when they should be picking up the bargains.

One might suppose from this that a simple formula of acting in a contrary manner would make it easy to rake in the profits.

However, those traits of human nature have to be dealt with, and they are obstinate obstructionists indeed! Above all, what makes it practically impossible to beat the game is the trait of IMPATIENCE.

THE PROBLEM OF KNOWING AND MEASURING OPINIONS

No problem connected with the Theory of Contrary Opinion is more difficult to solve than the one mentioned in the headline: (a) how to know what prevailing general opinions are; and (b) how to measure their prevalence and intensity.

Many ideas have come to me, and have been suggested to me, over the years, but I still find myself gauging opinions (and guessing at the correct contrary conclusion) from extensive reading and checking of newspapers, magazines, and numerous bulletins and letters.

Obviously, this is not scientific and might lead frequently to what a corresponding friend calls "mental mirror reflections." That is, one mistakenly considers himself in the minority and in consequence, exaggerates the views contrary to his own; yet, he may simply be exaggerating the majority viewpoint because he has misread his own thinking.

But I suppose it is true of any "thinking system" (if I dare use such an expression) that one must discipline his own mind if he intends to apply the system to his comments, discussions, and conclusions. Also, we have to recognize our mental shortcomings and allow for them in using any thinking method. I know in my case I have to go over thoughts and ideas to get them in mind (and frequently no doubt miss pertinent reasoning because my thinking through lacks sufficient depth) .

In sum, if you employ the method of scanning opinions you have to continually ask yourself: Is this truly a generalized viewpoint, or is it perhaps a composite of my own views which the "mirror" misleads me to think are those of the "crowd"?

A drawback in reading comments to obtain "opinions" is that prominent businessmen are likely to express what they *wish to have thought of as their beliefs*—even if their comments belie their true thoughts. It is not that executives wish to mislead people, but that they have uppermost in their minds the policy of putting their best foot forward. (Can one squeeze more clichés into one sentence!) So you have to make allowances as you survey—all quite unscientific and guessy—but where is the solution?

THE LAW OF MENTAL UNITY OF CROWDS

Demonstrations of "crowd behaviorism" were conspicuous and well-advertised in the Little Rock segregation issue. The emotional outbursts from the Little Rock *calamity of haste* cover the range of name calling, mob violence, and group braggadocio —manifestations of The Law of Mental Unity of Crowds.

As we know from our readings in crowd psychology a "crowd" has different characteristics from individuals. Individuality becomes lost, as it were, and a collective mind is formed. Le Bon (in *The Crowd —A Study of the Popular Mind*) states that a gathering thus becomes "an organized crowd ... it forms a single being, and is subjected to the Law of the Mental Unity of Crowds."

It perhaps need not be added that to come under this "law" a crowd requires a cause to incite the group with a unified purpose. Thousands of people may gather without their becoming a "crowd" from the psychological point of view. As Le Bon further explains: "A crowd is at the mercy of external exciting causes and reflect their incessant variations. It is the slave of the impulses which it receives."

A crowd becomes, as we saw in Little Rock, stirred up, excited, agitated, or even inflamed, in accordance with the degree of emotionalism which is contained in the subject matter that set off the wrangle or conflict in the first place.

Obviously, no more inflammatory subject could be imagined than the racial question, especially when a solution to the problem has been effected by legalistic methods, rather than by seeking out a possible basis for a meeting of adverse minds. Le Bon warns us about this, too, remarking that "ideas, sentiments, and customs are not to be recast by recasting legislative codes."

Unhappily, we witnessed in Little Rock what above I call "a calamity of haste." This emotional crowd conflict was brought about, it seems to me, by those who either were unmindful of crowd behaviorism or who simply were determined to show their muscle regardless of the consequences. In other words, we witnessed individuals acting as impetuously as crowds; or you might say that the leaders on both sides of the controversy joined in the mental unity of the crowds on their side. I cannot see that cither the Governor or the President acted with the calmness and foresight that is requisite in handling such an explosive problem.

If a "law" of contrary deliberations were recognized, the Little Rock affair would not have reached the stages it did. Adding to the contagious inflammation, were comments and editorials which unnecessarily took sides in a conflict about which many wrote merely emotionally. A point in favor of insisting upon a consideration of contrary viewpoints, in all important questions, is that it compels deliberation and forestalls headlong actions.

THE THEORY OF C. O. IS NOT A SYSTEM OF FORECASTING: IT IS A METHOD OF WORK ING TOWARD THOUGHT-OUT CONCLUSIONS

Not to tire you with too many additional whys and wherefores of the Theory of Contrary Opinion, yet I do want to argue out one or two aspects, because

1. The *useable* features of the Theory work out in practice and offer considerable promise as "think stimulators":
2. Yet, others who are writing or referring to Contrary Opinions (quite frequently of late) in most instances interpret them (in my view) incorrectly.

Only the other day a writer I know rather intimately remarked that the only time to follow contrary opinion is twice each cycle—near the tops and bottoms. Read hurriedly, it sounds all right, but of course one need not bother with any theories of economic analysis if he knows *when* he arrives at tops and bottoms!

It is (to be contrary) because no one CAN pinpoint tops and bottoms of cycles, whether they be stock-market cycles or any other cycle, that the theory of contrary analysis is useful.

To repeat the heading above: The Theory of C. O. is NOT a system of forecasting; but rather it is a method of working toward thought-out conclusions.

It is fallacious to think you can call the Theory into action every few months or years and by then going "contrary" suddenly make a number of brilliant decisions. You have to work up to your decisions, deliberately.

The purpose in using the "opposite approach" is to think through a given problem, or to gain thereby a fresh and different approach to a solution.

A point I've stressed before is, I think, te.nable: Contrary considerations compel deliberation and forestall headlong decisions.

It is my (long-experienced) contention that .the idea of considering contrary "angles"—when trying to determine a course of action—should be in *constant* use, if it is to prove practicable.

Contrary thinking becomes a useable and profitable habit only through constant practice. You cannot pull it out of a hat, or turn to it as a crystal ball, on those occasions when you're befuddled over coming consequences of a given event. If you do, I'll wager you will find that what you impulsively took to be contrary viewpoints are in reality majority opinions, because you interpreted them unconsciously in accordance with your own views.

Contrary opinions do not forecast, but they do check others' forecasts!

As I have argued so often in the past, contrary opinions are a wonderful sedative for overprophesying.

"WHY DO YOU THINK YOU THINK?"

With satellites and rockets flying about in spaceabove and beyond ordinary man's comprehensionyou begin to wonder if we here in America *think. enough.* I'm sure I don't; do you?

The Theory of Contrary Opinion is obviously a method of thinking. There have been numerous books on "how to think." I even had the effrontery to write one myself, "The Art of Contrary Thinking." Yes, I've given a lot of thought to thinking, and I truly believe it is a national necessity to foster more thinking and less "hearsaying." You know what I mean; the habit of remarking, when some question arises, *They* say so-and-so." (See page 193.)

In Ayn Rand's wonderful new book, *Atlas Shrugged,* she has one of her characters read aloud to himself from "Why Do You Think You Think?" His mind benumbed by the do-gooders and welfarestaters this fictional scientist reads, "Thought is a primitive superstition. Reason is an irrational idea. The childish notion that we are able to think has been mankind's costliest error. . . ." and so on. There are other dialogues and colloquies that are gems. Don't miss this grand book.

I often wonder, as I read discussions on modern education, why thinking is not taken up in schools. Even "contrary thinking" might be stimulating to teach!

For instance, one can investigate in the field of "fallacies." Noteworthy pamphlets and books on fallacies in monetary economics and in stock-market parlance have been published. Stuart Chase put out

Guides to Straight Thinking that encompasses 13 "principal fallacies or types of false reasoning," which is worth your time for reading. You'll find similar readings in the *Encyclopaedia Britannica* (but who ever thinks of *reading the Britannica?*).

LET US BE CONTRARY: LET US NOT DENY THAT OUR DESTINY LIES IN THE SKIES

You may not feel compelled to alter your own way of living to any great extent because of the rocket era (although investmentwise you'll need to), but you assuredly will feel compelled to make others perceive how essential it is for them to "get wise" to the *UNKNOWN* stretching before us.

Doubtless you've queried your friends about it, since Sputnik went aloft and our reading has been filled with our educational shortcomings and Russia's startling advances. Not long ago at a dinner gathering, among which were two secondary school administrators, I asked how long it would he before curriculums would be changed to advance our schooling in keeping with the scientific age.

Well, sir, before answers to the specific question could be heard there was a babble around the table that darn near put me under the table! "Do we wish to get narrow-minded like the Reds, and lose culture in order to gain submarines and rockets?" . . . and so on and so forth. Finally, in a momentary lapse, I asked, "Do you mean to tell me that no one at this table is frightened at what the Russians might do; that no one admits the narrow-minded Reds might annihilate us while we're enjoying our advanced culture and backward minds?" I needn't tell you what they did to me. I was simply that poor contrary boob who is carried away by Russian propaganda.

One of the angles in the Theory of Contrary Opinion calls for especially investigating subjects or events of which the general public (the "crowd") has little or no knowledge. You will recall how we stressed this in urging the study of "money" because so few people have any conception of monetary economics and how it influences trends.

In this case we're urging an acquaintanceship with "scientific affairs." You needn't know how to make a rocket to know it can carry explosives. However you need to know that others have learned how to make bigger rockets than we have—and they may not be so careful how they handle them, either.

We learn from history that war, or defense-impelled industrialization, shortens developments literally by years. (Think of strides in mass production during World War I and airplane output in World War II.) It is obvious, I think, that "Curves" of Growth, Decadence, and Statics, will reveal startling shifts because of the hurry-up stimulation of the space age. . . . It seems to me the railroads are foredoomed to nationalization before many years, unless public sentiment forces a change in featherbedding and wage policies and economics forces more mergers. They are up against falling patronage and rising costs; yet must be kept rolling for reasons of security and survival. . . . Or to guess at another "shocking" change, we may see interest-free government bonds some day. The scientific expansion we're getting into, under Russian competition and the lash of survival fears (which inject an emotional factor), will undoubtedly cause additional monetary disorders as time passes; a cry will go up for non-interest-bearing government bonds (or in plain language, printingpress certificates). . . . Let us be contrary; let us not deny that our destiny lies in the skies.

CAPITALISM'S BASIC FACTOR: EARNING POWER

It has become noticeable in late years that a basic tenet of capitalistic enterprise is being overlooked in the chatter about inflation and in the scramble for inflation protection.

The earning power of Property and of individuals is fundamental for success in a capitalistic society.

I venture to make a special essay of this subject because it is also fundamental to the problem of inflation, contrary to what many may believe.

Take for an example the commonly thought-of inflation hedge of rentable housing (homes and apartments), which one mortgages to the hilt on the theory that he'll pay off the mortgage with cheaper dollars.

This sounds simple, but there's a catch in it.

Various things happen to upset this "perfect" hedge during a rapid inflation. Rentals cannot be raised fast enough to keep ahead of maintenance and repairs; prices of property fall instead of rise be- cause the yield (earning power) *shrinks*. One has a losing proposition added to his loss from inflation. Mortgage liabilities become heavy for the same reason: low earning power. (You have to *earn* the cheaper dollars; they do not *sprout* merely because of the inflation!) To cap it off, in a real inflation the government will be sure to step in and clap a ceiling on rents in order to protect the "little fellow," and those living on fixed incomes. Taxes become a frightful burden also as the "state" scrambles to get in more money as the currency-depreciation progresses.

Common stocks are popular inflation hedges among those who have some knowledge of such things (but only a relatively small minority of younger people are sufficiently familiar with investment principles to speculate in stocks during an inflation, and another vast group haven't the means to buy stocks).

Many stocks will prove to be poor hedges because during the inflation their *earning power* drops. Numerous companies fail in fast inflations. You cannot stick a pin through the financial page and say, "I'll take this one for my hedge." Both the French and German inflations reflected the difficulties in using domestic stocks as hedges. It is well to remember that *profits* are mighty tough to earn in a fast inflation, or for that matter in a persistent inflation.

Commodities make good hedges, but how many people have facilities for holding commodities? . . . Perhaps the essential point has been made that *earning Power (of property and of individuals) is fundamental in successfully combating losses from a deteriorating currency.* Land, for instance, judged to have *future attraction and earning probabilities* is an excellent hedge (if free and clear and not subject to unfair assessments).

A LIBERTARIAN SURELY HAS TO BE A CONTRARIAN THESE DAYS!

There are not many articles in today's magazines that a libertarian bothers to clip and preserve. Most of the current commentaries seem to me to be slanted either leftward or apologetically. By the latter I mean that those essays which start out with a forceful right-wing punchline often shade off and become almost apologetic in tone.

So it was that you can imagine my pleasure in reading Miss Edith Hamilton's thrilling "The Lessons of the Past" in the *Saturday Evening Post* of September 27, 1958.

There is need only to quote one paragraph to give you the gist of the article, but perhaps I'd better first remind you that the late Miss Hamilton was an authority on Greek and Roman civilizations concerning which she wrote several books, including *The Greek Way* and *The Roman Way* (only fifty cents each, in paper covers).

Writing at 91 (yes, ninety-one) she penned a few words that we might wake up before it is too late.

Remarking that to be able to be caught up into the world of thought—is to be educated," Miss Hamilton emphasizes that the Athenian method of education was not geared to mass production. It did not produce people who instinctively all went in one way, and were conformists. There were countless contrarians in Greece back in Socrates' day. You can imagine some of the answers Socrates would get if he were making street-corner stops today. But let me get to the paragraph I want you to clip and carry in your billfold to pass around the dinner table. To quote Miss Hamilton:

> Is it rational that now when the young people rnay have to face problems harder than we face, is it reasonable that with the atomic age before them, at this time we are giving up the study of how the Greeks and Romans prevailed magnificently in a barbaric world: the study, too, of how that triumph ended, how a slackness and a softness finally came over them to their ruin? In the end, more than they wanted freedom, they wanted security, a comfortable life, and they lost all—security and comfort and freedom.

So saying, she asks: "Is that not a challenge to us?"

THE FALLACY IN ECONOMIC
EXTRAPOLATION

(Extrapolate: To project by inference into an unexplored situation from observations in an explored field, on assumption of continuity or correspondence.—*Webster's New Collegiate Dictionary.*)

I find that the word "extrapolation" becomes more and more popular among the erudite and professional economists, so I think we might discuss it in relation to the theory of contrary opinion. (The definition is included in the heading for the convenience of many of you who, as I do, run to the dictionary when you run across these professorial-sounding words.)

Let me say at once that *statistical*, as distinct from economic, extrapolation is of real advantage and in common use. (E.g. You can usefully project such "futures" as the birth rate, by taking an average thought to represent a similar period.)

I should say that the distinction when and when not to trust extrapolation would arise when the *human* factor is involved. That is, when people have to decide something—as opposed to the more or less regular rhythms of numerous occurrences. I hold one goes out on the guessy limb when he extrapolates from an observation o from what happens to be occurring in "crowd activities."

Countless forecasts (I'd be willing to assert that the *majority* of predictions) are made largely upon projecting into the future what is happening in the present. Today's trends are expected to continue tomorrow and into next week.

That it is a fallacy to rely upon extrapolation in making *economic* forecasts becomes evident, I believe, when you stop to realize that

> what IS occurring at any given time may be the cause of a complete shift and reversal of the extrapolated trends. Obviously, this is witnessed in the revolutions of the business cycle: a boom brings on a bust (or used to!) and the lesser gyrations.

What put me in mind to write this piece was a letter from a professor in the school of business administration in one of larger Midwestern universities. I had written to him that youngish people as a whole were not much interested in the theory of contrary opinion: to which he replied that "basically, of course, young people are optimistic . .. and fondly extrapolate the buoyancy of the present. They are not prepared to face a downturn because they view society as an extension of themselves." (What an interesting observation from one who is in daily contact with young economic and business students! Thanks again Dr. S.)

There is a lot to ruminate over in the above, isn't there? For one thing, thousands of young executives have never experienced an all-out depression.

HOW TO LOOK AHEAD — PROFITABLY

I think the reason we peer ahead with such unprofitable accuracy is explainable; moreover it seems to me there may be a remedy.

With the aid of the accompanying simple sketch I shall now endeavor to show you the Neill system for forward thinking! It is not copyrighted. You have full rights to it, with the understanding that there is no guarantee of results!

Now we'll get to the point of the system.

You will agree, will you not, that the common method of looking ahead is to assume that what is now happening is likely to continue in the same manner?

This is termed "extrapolation" as we previously mentioned—a fifty-cent word which, if we understand it, is worth a great deal more!

To extrapolate means, in non-technical language, to calculate ahead from conditions as they exist in the present. (Or see definition, page 168.)

The system calls for a three-step procedure, as follows:

1. Establish the extrapolation (e.g., the current stock-market trend is up, therefore it will continue up).
2. Consider all conditions and qualifications that come to mind which conflict with, or nullify, the idea that trends will continue to run on as in the present. (Down if up, and vice versa.)
3. Thirdly, think of motivations or circumstances that might activate trends to a greater degree than presently prevail.

(E.g., the popular extrapolation in early January, 1959, was that "everything" would go along moderately well; thus a contrary opinion would also be that there would be an upsurge of greater proportions than expected, which there was.)

You may be saying to yourself that this system is not going to help very much because how will one know which of the contra-opinions to go by?

Whereat I rudely reply, "That is what our heads are for, to figure out which direction to take at forks in the road. Which is certainly smarter than remaining on a road that you know must reach a dead end if you don't turn off."

In any event, this system will exercise your mind and prevent brain atrophy.

IS THERE ANY REAL PURPOSE IN CONTRARY THINKING?

Every so often in my writings I cannot resist repeating myself on the usefulness of the Theory of Contrary Opinion.

One learns from experience as well as from books. And you learn most of all, perhaps, from writing on a subject and from teaching it.

I have been writing steadily on the subject of the Contrary Theory since 1940, and prior to that my reading and activities were slanted directly at the *human side* of finance and socioeconomics. That is, it was the foibles and fancies of us humans that interested me far more than the cold statistical appraisals. The famous '29 crash and window-jumping era supplied plenty of fodder for early cud chewing.

In such a period of time you are sure to learn something, especially when your readers come back at you and debate your theses.

The chief "catch" in the C.O. Theory seems to be that readers persist in looking upon it as a forecasting tool or system, whereas, in actuality, it is an antidote to careless and fruitless predictions. It prevents one, if he adopts it, from trying to predict the unpredictable.

Basically, the theory merely calls for getting into the habit of asking queries, such as, "Suppose the opposite is true, then what?" "Some say this and some say that; is there a third probability, presently unthought of?" "The 'crowd' is usually 'right' during the early stages of a craze or trend but as the crowd will hang on too long, is the 'terminal point' close at hand?"

The starting point for *contrary* thinking is the popular thought or opinion of the moment. However, if popular opinions swing about, it follows that we have to go off on another track for contrary calculations. Consistency is not possible when opinions and public whims change with every fresh news event or trial balloon.

Let me illustrate with a communication from a reader. He argues for a *positive* contrary opinion at all times, whereas it may be necessary to straddle when opinions are a stand-off. At such times the situation is a "stalemate." I perhaps over-play my objection to dogmatism but being cocksure over suppositions is not sound practice.

Yes, I think there is indeed a real purpose in contrary thinking and I trust you are finding it so. It takes a little time to adopt the practice, but it's worth it.

LIMBERING UP YOUR MIND

May I emphasize the thought that "contrary thinking" is one of the best ways to limber up your mind; and I hope you'll try it out. You've noticed how, at a school or college baseball game, the coach has the ball batted around the bases to limber up the infield, before the team gets down to the business of scoring runs, hits, put-outs, and errors.

You can limber up your mind the same wayby tossing ideas back and forth. Countless creative ideas have been originated by one idea bringing to mind another. You can enhance the game by throwing in contrary ideas. There is nothing like disagreements to bring out fresh thought. Try batting the ball around the next time you have a problem to solve. Toss in all the contrary angles you think of. You will find this pro and con method most helpful in rounding out the information you require for a sound solution.

A MONEY-MIND VERSUS THE IMPETUOUS IMPULSE TO MAKE SOME EASY MONEY

An article in the April (1961) issue of *Cosmopolitan* prompts a repeat discussion of a favorite topic of the Ruminator's; namely, success comes from your mind, never alone from books. The theory of contrary opinion enters the equation also.

The title of the article mentioned is "Can Reading a Book Make You Rich?" Photographs, one large one in color, display a number of the many books that have been published in recent lush times on making big money in stocks, real estate, and salesmanship. There, but for the grace of second thought, might have been a Neill make-yourself-rich-book. A prominent publisher was interested some time ago in a book by this writer on the thesis of the "money mind." I say "but for the grace of second thought" because when first suggested I thought of doing it . . . but as soon as I put some ideas on paper, in readiness for the task, I realized such a book would be little more than a potboiler that might mislead people into actually believing that getting-rich-quick was merely a matter of following the directions on the wrapper! I quickly dropped the matter and filed the notes.

Success books have been much in demand especially since the advent of the last two bull markets. I read the other day of a newstand proprietor who said that sales of financial publications and how-to-beat-the-market books were so brisk he couldn't keep them in stock . . . whereas he remembered that ten years ago he could not move the stuff off his shelves. An interesting comparison of 1961 with 1951.

There isn't space to review the *Cosmopolitan* article, but it's worth reading for its timeliness and its indirect warning that we may be on the brink of, if not already in, a mania for wealth-withoutworking (that can only end in disappointments and flattened pocketbooks—as it did in May-June, 1962). I have referred to similar manifestations as noted in the over-size, tip-language advertisements in the financial press (which, by the way, I see the SEC intends to restrain) , and in the chart-reading craze.

About the money-mind versus an impetuous impulse to make some easy money, let me explain briefly what is meant by the wording.

By money-mind I refer to the type of mental apparatus a few are endowed with that leads them as a matter of course to think of the *money side* in every conversation, in every endeavor or transaction engaged in. The average person, on the other hand, seldom thinks of money except, of course, when he or she is spending money or planning to spend it, or when a new job or contract is in view.

The money-minded person is constantly on the lookout for ways to make money. At the same time he is usually a well-balanced individual so he does not blast off in reckless undertakings. He thinks out the money angles: probabilities for losses as well as for profits. He considers the risks in terms of the probabilities for success.

At times, such as the present—April, 1961— thousands of persons become temporarily infected with the money-making bug—it is very catching when people all around you are talking of the money they're making. However, background and experience seldom justify their impetuous impulses for trying to make some easy money. A money-mind is a trained mind whereas impetuous impulses spring from a *lack* of money sense.

A money-mind employs contrary opinions to guard against impetuous actions.

COMMUNISTS PRACTICE THE THEORY OF C.O.

The Communists are conspicuous in contrary thought and action. The zigzag tactics within the strategy of prolonged conflict are "contrary actions." They have been found successful, for their purposes —but one would suppose the "West" would be able to confound this use of contrary tactics now that they have become so well recognized.

As you observe communist actions it becomes apparent that when the Reds are confronted with a problem concerning 'Wrest-East relationships they sit down and conjure up all the *probable steps* the West is likely to take and then figure out as many *opposite responses and procedures* as they can.

Battle tactics of course follow similar principles: to be where the enemy expects you aren't and *to do the unexpected.*

One of the "fixed" habits of us Western humans (not apparently the same with the Oriental mind) is to assume that what is transpiring now will continue to occur in a similar mariner "tomorrow and the next day." We find it most difficult to expect *change*—and almost impossible to expect the unexpected!

If Khrushchev has been offensive and overbearing in two or three public appearances it is expected that he will be equally nasty in his next appearance. We, on the other hand, are inclined to remain more or less in the same paltern in our dealings with others. We practice common courtesies.

> We have to accept, in the protracted conflict we are engaged in, that our adversaries will never act as we do, or as we might expect them to. We must learn to counter their contrary tactics, if we hope to win the Cold War.

Instincts of the Herd in Peace & War, by Wilfred Trotter, was first published in 1916, and therein we read that "man's suggestibility is not the abnormal casual phenomenon it is often supposed to be, but a normal instinct present in every individual . . ."

Mr. Trotter stresses the gregarious nature of man and how it leads him astray. (Today, gregariousness is called "togetherness!") We are reminded that "if we examine the mental furniture of the average man, we shall find it made up of a vast number of judgments of a very precise kind upon subjects of very great variety, complexity, and difficulty." (This further reminds us of the wisecrack: Often in error, but never in doubt.) Trotter further asserts that the bulk of such (widespread) opinions must necessarily be

without rational basis, since many are con- cerned with unsolved problems, "while to the rest it is clear that the training and experience of the average man can qualify him to
have no opinion upon them at all . . . (thus) this wholesale
acceptance of non-rational belief must be looked upon as
normal." To which we add, thus the value of *contrary opinions.*

THE RIGHT WORD (OR THOUGHT) MAY BE
WORTH A THOUSAND PICTURES

You continually run across the saying—A Picture is
Worth a Thousand Words. Attributed to the Chinese
philosophers, it probably was coined in Chinatown, U.S.A.

Like so many mouthings, it is only true when both the
picture and the words are qualified. As commonly used it
is false.

Many devotees of chart reading, for forecasting stock
prices, subscribe to the idea that a chart is worth a thousand
words of analysis and statistics. Permit me to twist this
around. I maintain "the right contact is worth a thousand
charts."

Anyone who has observed the speculative fireworks that
have illuminated Wall Street environs over the past few
years will agree, I think, that *knowing the right people—having
profitable "Street" connections* —has been far more advantageous than keeping a thousand charts up to date.

Perhaps I should quickly inject that I am not opposed to the intelligent use of charts. They have
their worthwhile usages, especially as checker-up-

pers to preconceived ideas or tips. It is the "depend-all" form of chart usage I'm afraid of. (I regularly receive the excellent chart books, as I've mentioned, from the Securities Research Corp., 211 Congress St., Boston, which give one a background of weekly and monthly price changes *plus* earnings' curves and financial data.)

When any "movement" or "system" becomes a VOGUE it is contagious and soon followed by the Crowd. Then contrarians recall an admonition of Sir Francis Bacon: "Watch your idols! Doubt all before you believe. . . ." Chart reading has indeed become an idolatrous pastime—and naturally so as numerous stock prices have enjoyed extraordinary advances, which stand out in stilt fashion on the charts. Then, too, the Darvas book on getting-richquick (now in a paperback edition!) was a ringing commercial for chart reading.

As the Ruminator ventured to suggest a fortnight ago, when charts are used the most is the time to be most careful how you use them.

To go back a moment, I grant that "right contacts" are difficult to cultivate. However, *if one has enough interest* he can develop contacts that will prove profitable. I know a chap who doesn't hesitate to pick up the telephone and call the President of a likely concern in some distant city to ask straight-out: "How are things going?" Of course, my inquiring friend previously studies the company, conjectures on its prospects, and familiarizes himself with the financial setup. In other words, he goes about it intelligently, not haphazardly. He finds officials of the lesser-known organizations are usually happy to discuss business with those who are sincere and interested in the company's shares. Similarly with calling in person on prospects you may pick up in your conversations. Another friend of mine makes it a practice to drop in on establishments whose shares have attraction, or may someday "go public."

A THINK-IT-OUT-FOR-YOURSELF KIT

I feel the need for a think-kit, don't you? You know to what I refer: something like the do-ityourself kits we see advertised. Or, maybe what we need is a geiger counter for the mind that will detect fresh thoughts!

We can utilize the Contrary Theory as the tool to gather our thoughts together.

We are all familiar with the practice of "association of ideas" which is employed in the art of creativity. Creating ideas seldom springs from new or original thoughts. The fresh ideas come from one idea suggesting another—in a chain reaction.

Contrary thinking accomplishes this most profitably. I have been taken by surprise by events which, if my think-kit had been operating properly, would not have caught me off guard.

The trick is to observe, and to concentrate, on "counter angles" in the news and commentaries and in the myriad of predictions that bombard us.

I think various discussions I had in late 1961 in reference to the "climax hypothesis" illustrates what I'm driving at. As the talk of crisis and of war continued to mount last fall—the President accented it (and rightfully, I think)—it finally struck me a counter blow and I said to myself, there must be an end to this mounting peril *sometime*: either by a nuclear holocaust or by a climax to the Cold -War.

November 1961 registered a high point in war fears. I discussed it at that time, in rather sober LETTERS, I remember. Whether there is any connection may be debatable, but the stock market registered its high point of the bull market in November also.

I continue on the sharp lookout for indications of a *climax* to the protracted communist conflict, because world conditions appear to be shifting.

Right here, perhaps, is a good place to remind readers who have not had an opportunity to become "contrary minded" that others will often disagree (sometimes violently!) with your contrary viewpoints.

In November, 1961, when I openly discussed the pessimism over war fears that were then prevalent, I was raked over the coals by an advisory sheet that is given to heated comments. The sheet in question scoffed at any idea of caution or pessimism—even went so far as to declaim that "investors will wonder whatever got into their heads when they sold prime growth equities in the fall of 1961." Mind you, this was in a November issue—the same month the stock market registered its "high days," under excited trading volume. I had signed off my November first LETTER, with "That's how dreary it looks from Vermont," because I regretted having written sobering comments. The advisory sheet in question couldn't stand this and asserted that this unfortunate contrarian from Vermont "had been bumped off his trolley and is out in left field flapping with the fumblewits." Now there's literary composition for you! You see what you get when you're contrary. (Yet, those growth equities were the "stumble stocks" of '61 and were soon off huge percentages from their highs in the spring of 1961.) Oh, well, every man to his taste. I miss too many targets to aim shafts at others.

OPINIONS AND WORDS VERSUS FACTS

The Ruminator was reminded by an interesting communication that we need occasionally to stress the subject of opinions versus facts.

It was especially important in April, 1962, be- cause of the overflowing of wordage in the public prints—on all manner of subjects from economics to aerodynamics, electronics, and the climactics of the Cold War. (Between the "isms" and "ics" we are being driven mad by suffixes!)

As the above-mentioned communication warned. "it is of utmost importance in using the Theory of C.O. to be contrary to *words* and not to facts. It is words that mislead, distort, and delude. To be contrary to words is a most wise and often profitable practice, but to be contrary to facts (although a universal habit of the Crowd and others who should know better) is to invite disaster."

I quote my correspondent because of the clear manner of expression. (I might add that his war service was with the Military Intelligence and he had experiences that bear out his remarks I have quoted.)

Opinions are expressed in words and are the result of words. So it is a helpful idea to have the foregoing comment which puts the emphasis on WORDS.

The term WORDS at once suggests another term, PROPAGANDA. This latter practice has become one of the deceptive and illusive usages of the post-depression, war, and postwar years. It would be impossible to estimate the extent that "canned" news (otherwise known as "releases") influences opinions and the actions of Crowds. Because of the world crisis we are undergoing a constant barrage of *words* that "mislead, distort, and delude."

The safeguard is contrary analysis and contrary opinions.

Moreover—contrary watchfulness is required in reading statements and business releases. Obviously, businessmen are not going to put a bad face on their remarks about their company and its operations, if they can avoid it. If a businessman asserts that the earnings of his company fell sharply, it is a reflection on his administration of the business. Therefore, if he has to report poor profits you may be sure he will quickly point out that such-and-such conditions forced a loss upon his company (through no fault in management, being implied) .

In the old days, businessmen might give out bad reports in order to unsettle their shares on the Exchange so they and their friends could pick up some undervalued stock. But this practice is pretty well done away with today. However, what we do witness today is the cheerful exhortation of a company's well-being at luncheon meetings of Analysts'

Societies. These bits of happy propaganda likewise require an equal amount of contrary questioning.

As the deadlock of the Cold War continues, contrary opinions will most certainly help us to escape the delusions of the times. We must guard against the propagandist who believes his own lies, as my correspondent remarked.

THE YEARS FORECASTERS WOULD LIKE TO FORGET

There have been many years when forecasts have gone wrong. But perhaps recent years have witnessed more wrong guesses than usual.

What put me in mind of this was a front-page story in the New York Herald Tribune of June 19, 1962, headed "The Year Economists Would Rather Forget, and Why." We are much indebted to the writer, Joseph R. Slevin, National Economics Editor of the Herald Trib, for his documented argument for the Neill Theory of Contrary Opinion. When our thesis rates first-page treatment (boxed, no less, across five columns) in a metropolitan newspaper, I am sure you will agree that there is something significant in the C.O. thinking system.

Mr. Slevin introduced his article with the words: "This is the year [1962] of the big economic surprise. The experts have been confounded, and there's not an unshattered crystal ball left in Washington."

It strikes me that doubting Contrarians can take their cue from that introduction. When crystal balls are shattered it clearly means that those who *thought* opposite to the experts were on the right forecasting tack.

The article in question follows the events of the half-year, demonstrating, as the writer asserts, that both businessmen and government policy-makers "have to stay flexible—for they can't tell what's coming next."

We might argue a bit with Mr. Slevin on that last remark. 'While we are quick to agree that predicting what's-to-come-next is loaded with risks, nevertheless taking a contrary position, will frequently suggest what is NOT coming next. By thinking through the "opposites" one can make a fair stab at guessing what *might* be coming next. At least, one can fortify himself against the unexpected, and that is a great gain over being "confounded" and having your crystal ball shattered.

With our reading packed solid with opinions and predictions, it is a wonder if the average person ever makes sensible decisions. He is pulled in one direction most of the time—and most of the time the direction is the wrong one. As this Ruminator has so frequently mentioned, the *sameness* of writings on business, finance, and economics—and of course on the stock market—is such that it is almost impossible for an individual to think for himself. He is brainwashed.

The protection against brainwashing is contrary brain*work*. It is hard work to think, but it is worth it.

As we look ahead into the second half of the confounding year of 1962, let us adopt the plan of mentally checking everything we read. If Washington experts appear before our television screens with brave predictions of things to come, let us not forget that they are there to *persuade us to think their way.* The open-mouth policy is a scheduled phase of modern government. For protection against the unexpected, therefore, be contrary!

QUICK TO CONFORM, BUT SLOW TO DIFFER

We are all subject to curious traits in thinking —and we are all prone at one moment to hop onto ideas without thinking, while at other times we cling to our opinions although we know down inside we're probably wrong.

There is one noticeable trait—a paradox—that is pertinent to today's trends of opinions:

> a) A person is commonly slow to change his mind, while being
>
> b) Quick to pounce on a new fad or shift to a new fashion.
>
> Which is to say we are quick to conform, but slow to differ.

When one is in the process of changing his mind, he needs *time* to think things through. It seldom pays to jump to conclusions, because the leap usually lands us just where everybody else is standing.

Under the Theory of Contrary Opinion, if everybody seems to be of the same mind, we contrarians opine otherwise.

At the moment (October 15, 1962), "everybody" is pretty downcast and discouraged when viewing the stock market. Nobody is interested in buying stocks (although apparently everyone is eager to buy a new automobile. Is the auto again to be a status symbol?).

From a Wall Street viewpoint, the odds now favor *the patient bull* on two counts:

1. The bears are more numerous and are getting careless;
2. Large numbers of the public have been driven out of the market, or have left in disgust.

There will be jerks and false starts—to traders' further dismay—but if there is validity in the Theory of C.O. the time has come to shift our minds around to a constructive outlook. As discussed above, a shift of this kind is never easy to accomplish. One likes to cling to his previous opinions.

However, bearishness and apprehension are about as universal as they ever get; so the time has come to think constructively —and less defensively.

FORTY-ONE YEARS OF "UNEXPECTED" EVENTS

I'm sometimes asked about unexpected (and unsuspected) events of the past, when contrary ruminating might have been useful in mental preparedness and when contrary planning might have saved losses to nations as well as to peoples. Here are a few; many more might be added.

1914   Little general appre-
       hension of war. News-
       papers carried scarcely
       any mention of strained
       relations prior to midJuly,
       1914.

Yet—black headlines soon ap-
peared:
Aug. 1—Germany Declares
War on Russia
Aug. 2—Germany Invades
France
Aug. 4—Germany Invades Bel-
gium
Aug. 5—England Declares War
   on Germany

A stunned world looked on unbelieving

1916   Sensational rise in stocks
       of "war babies" and gen-
       eral stockmarket boom
       expected to continue.

Year-long bear market set in in
November, 1916. By December,
1917, market average almost returned full cycle.

1919   Immediate postwar de-
       pression generally ex-
       pected and predicted.

Inflation boom occurred, to be
nicknamed the "silk shirt era."

1926   Fears of another bear
       market and depression.

"New Era" commenced, with
greatest market rise in history.

1929   Permanent plateau of
       prosperity.

New Era delusions shattered.

1930's Economics: We reached
       the age of "maturity."
       World Politics: Why
       worry about the little pa-
       perhanger and h i s Nazis?

Economic maturity laughable,
but Hitler no laughing mat¬ter!
War in 1939 expected but "it
can't last long." Hitler "has no
money and no powerful armies."

1940   Hitler could never breach
       famed French Maginot
       line; Holland's dikes
       would be opened to flood
       out any invader. The stock
       market was expected to
       rise when the invasion oc-
       curred on May 10 to 14,
       1940.

The "blitzkrieg" overran Belgium, Holland, and into France
as fast as the reports carried the
news. The west¬ern world awoke
to the realization that "everybody's" opinion about Hitler and
the Nazi armies was woefully
wrong! The market collapsed on
the fall of France.

1945-1946	Immediate postwar slump expected, with eight to twelve million to be unemployed.	As in 1919, a postwar "replacement" boom made all predictions look silly.
1949	Great Britain would not again devalue the pound, Sir Stafford Cripps so asserting some thirteen times.	September 18, pound devalued to $2.80; currencies of 29 other nations following suit—and as many more since.
1947-1954	Persistent predictions of a slump were common.	Booming conditions largely prevailed; there were only brief interruptions.
1955-1957	The years when fears of slumps vanished and the idea of perpetual prosperity became the fad.	Stock market collapsed in mid-'57 just when the future looked brightest.
1961	Mania for growth. Stocks fomented a great speculative era; hundreds of companies "went public"; and a greedy public grabbed for the shares at fast-rising prices.	As in manias of the past, the cruel awakening came in the summer of '62, as stock prices plunged. Again, it paid to be contrary!

And so we come to the end of our narratives and essays on THE ART OF CONTRARY THINKING.

The writer's hope is that you, the reader, will fol¬low through with persistent thinking on the Theory of Contrary Opinion to the end that it may develop into *clearer* thinking on the world's intense and complex subjects.

EPILOGUE

SLAVES TO "THEY"
by
SAMUEL B. PETTENGILL

The Honorable Samuel B. Pettengill has a Vermont background going back to the eighteenth century. After graduation
from Middlebury College and Yale Law School, Mr. Pettengill
practiced law in Indiana later becoming a member of Congress from 1931 to 1939 (where among other accomplishments he helped to defeat FDR's "court-packing bill").
Subsequently, he became an author of note (Smoke Screen
was a bestseller all during 1940). He wrote countless newspaper columns and conducted a forum on the air. Retiring in
1956, Mr. Pettengill returned to his home base, Grafton, Vermont—a neighboring village to Saxton's River. What follows
appeared as a "guest letter" for me when I went on vacation
. . . H. B. N.

Whether one owns a single share of stock or not, the
practice of contrary thinking is of growing importance because there is increasingly less of it.

The old-time editors, country lawyers and David Harums
have been laid away and their places taken by merged newspapers and centrally controlled nationwide television and
radio chains. Hungry for headlines, they join forces to magnify every quarrel between rival goat herdsmen into an international incident of grave importance to all mankind,
and to solve which all must unite.

My friend Humphrey's desire for brief surcease from cark and care gives me the opportunity to discuss this theme from several angles.

"Togetherness" has become a major curse because it inhibits individual thought. What do "they" think, or what will "they" wear? Females will not be caught dead wearing anything but the latest fashion made by garment designers who obsolete all clothes in order to sell new ones. So female skirts climb up and down, and males send practically new double-breasted suits to the ragman in response to the hidden persuaders of fashion.

Same with the fads in furniture, furnishings, jewelry, split-level ranch houses and the number of kids you should breed. What man of you is bold enough to put one of those truly comfortable old Morris chairs in your living room? Where are the rugged individualists of yesteryear? They have be- come slaves to "they."

In our public schools, the John-Deweyites and social adjusters have nearly made individuality a mortal sin. Schoolgirls weep bitterly if their "oldfashioned" mothers tell them that something would look better on their heads than the prevailing ponytails.

When a can of paint, mixed with cigarette stubs and decayed cockroaches, is heaved against a crumpled piece of old oilcloth, it is almost certain to get an award of hundreds of dollars as a new form of art from a committee of thin-chested savants whose "ipse dixit" is then beyond challenge.

Schoolteachers who have old-fashioned ideas about equipping a child with mental muscles to meet such of life's problems as go beyond the correct behavior at a beer joint, have to bootleg the three R's into their pupils' skulls, unbeknownst to their principal.

While at school, our poor little dears have few, if any, required subjects, examinations, or grades for excellence. They are huddled "together" in the lowest common denominator. Soft snaps are in fashion. The old-time disciplines of Latin and Algebra are gone with the wind, whereas the truth that *only from struggle comes strength* should be on every blackboard!

If as a humble taxpayer you even question the wisdom of making the breeding of bastards a profession through a system of welfare prizes for female fecundity, you are a "humanitarian" and are shunned in the best circles.

To promote the cult of the mass-man, greatness is downgraded and heroism not mentioned. A new two-volume history of the United States, 1075 pages long, published by the University of Michigan Press, does not have room to mention Nathan Hale, or the immortal Captain Lawrence ("Don't give up the ship"), or to quote the flaming words of John Paul Jones "I have just begun to fight."

Another recent history, *The American Past*, also has no room for John Paul Jones, but does find room for Mr. Jesse Jones, and says of Sacco and Vanzetti that they were "electrocuted on a trumped up murder charge," which is the author's opinion, but not history.

"They" have bulldozed the American people into believing the nonsense that a decision of the U.S. Supreme Court is "the supreme law of the land." The judges themselves don't think so. They all take an oath to support the supreme law of the land, but don't think they are breaking any such law when they reverse their own previous decisions. They know the Constitution vests *all* the legislative power it grants in Congress, and none in the court.

It is worth recalling that the Fugitive Slave Law of 1859 was held constitutional by the Supreme Court, but was denounced and disobeyed by leading citizens of the North. State legislatures pronounced it void. But then the shoe was on a different foot.

After following slogans and sloganeers during forty-three years of interventionism in foreign affairs, one would think it worth while to do a little contrary thinking in order to avoid sinking still deeper into our next bottomless bog. You might painfully recall the war to end war," or "make the world safe for democracy," or point out that by getting rid of the Kaiser we got Hitler, and then unhorsed Hitler and lifted Stalin into Hitler's saddle, and fed his horse.

But if you mention a recent President's liking for "good old Joe," you are sure to be shouted down by the one-worlders and togetherers as a benighted isolationist, who is dead but unburied.

Doesn't it sometimes strike you that we are biting off more than we can chew in the jungles of Darkest Africa? The white man's burden of Rudyard Kipling's time was nothing compared to the mess we are urging ourselves into. In Kipling's time, we were smart enough to let other nations carry the load. By taking Washington's and Jefferson's advice to mind our own business, we built a great country and had friends everywhere.

But now, fired by a holy zeal to save mankind from its own self-inflicted wounds, we march into the new vacuums of Asia and Africa singing "Onward U.N. soldiers" as the British, French, Dutch, and Belgian soldiers march out. As far as eye can see, Africa and Asia will now be in turmoil until shrimps whistle, and we will pay the bills. About all we ever get to see of the dove of peace is the *bill*!

Surely some contrary thinking as to the past, present, and future of our country might be useful.

Does any statesman of the West really burn any midnight oil over the problem of the population explosion that is taking place today—the world growing by 50,000,000 more mouths to feed each year, and these multiplying millions creating new hungers for land and raw materials?

Advancing science and agricultural techniques will, of course, mitigate these pressures, but that they will permanently solve them is doubtful indeed. Population experts tell us that there are *more hungry people in the world today than before foreign aid began*. The famous Malthusian Doctrine of 1798 looked wrong for a century because there were the immense areas of practically unpeopled land in the U.S.A., Canada, Australia, etc. But where is free land today? Not in China with 669,000,000 people, nor in India with 403,000,000, nor in Japan (a land no larger than California) with 100,000,000.

What kind of government, in fact, can cope with millions of hungry people except a police state? Take food away from any peaceful community (your own, for instance), for three days, and the law of the jungle takes over.

The human herd, like the Gadarene swine (Luke 5:13), loves to go stampeding off "together" after some real or imagined goal, and nearly always goes too far. It seems impossible that in the great Tulip Mania in Holland in 1640 the human herd could be such utter fools as to bid up tulip bulbs to 5500 florins each (equal to approximately $3,000) and crack a nation's banking system in the process. But so it is recorded in *Extraordinary Popular Delusions and the Madness of Crowds*, a book which Mr. Bernard Baruch says "saved him millions of dollars." And do you remember 1929?

And did it really happen in our lifetime that clergymen demanded "a life (sentence) for a pint"; and the confiscation of automobiles and the closing of huge hotels for what is now completely legal?

When mass manias are tied to a personality (Napoleon), patriotism (war), or God (the Crusades, or witchcraft), the hypnotic contagion of the crowd has no limits. It must wear itself out, as in the case of the Crusades, that took two hundred years (see stories in *Popular Delusions* mentioned above).

During the reign of Roosevelt II, his colossal stupidity in believing that Stalin was "a peace-loving democrat" infected the American mass to the point where, according to Gallup, 94% of us, after Yalta, had no doubt of his good intentions! No well-known book publisher would print any exposure of Roosevelt's folly. "They" would not like that.

Probably no one thing has damaged our country in world opinion today as much as our killing, without warning, of tens of thousands of non-combatant women and children at Hiroshima and Nagasaki. Yet who denounced it at the time? Only now has our government permitted us to learn that the Japanese had been trying to negotiate a surrender, but that we would not even talk with them. This deprived the bombing of all excuse and leaves us with the record of being the only nation in the world to have used the most barbaric of all weapons.

However, the hopeful thing about mankind's wild stampedes is that in time they do wear out. There is a law of the pendulum in human affairs. The native intelligence of the people finally does reassert itself, but only, may I add, because single individuals, here and there, *begin to speak up.* Note what happened to the Eighteenth Amendment.

As Jefferson said, *"We are never permitted to despair of the Commonwealth.* . . . A little patience and we shall see the reign of witches over. . . and the people recovering their true sight, restore their government to its true principles"!

If I did not have that faith, I would not have written this piece.

However, it does rile my customary good nature no end when I catch the hidden persuaders operating on me, as if I were Pavlov's dog. How sly they are, these "engineers of consent," these "conditional reflexers," these ((they." And how powerfully they apply their secret stimuli, armed with the new engines of mass communications. How they mark "classified" the documents they don't want you to see; hush the radio speaker they don't want you to hear, and refuse to publish books giving the other side of the question.

I'm against them, not only because they offend my sense of personal dignity, but because they are promoting a kind of totalitarianism—total control of the minds of men. It is the "group think" of Orwell's *Nineteen Eighty-Four.*

No one will claim that a contrary opinion is necessarily better than the prevailing opinion. Nor that a man should make a nuisance of himself by constantly quarreling with the opinions of others, or refuse to go along with a candidate or party because he objects to one or two out of fifty platform planks.

But in the still watches of the night, the habit of looking before leaping has been found useful by the few people—and nations—who've tried it!

Some years ago, a young Italian was being examined in a naturalization court. He was asked all the usual questions. But to clinch his right to be a citizen of this great Republic, the judge asked "How many stars are in the Flag?"

"Ninety-six, your Honor". . . A flag was hanging on the court room wall. The judge pointed to it and said, "Tony, can't you count?" . . "Yes, your Honor, but have you looked at both sides of the Flag?"

The young man passed. He had not been asked how many states were in the Union, but how many stars were in the Flag, and he had looked!

September, 1961

AFTERWORD
Reflections on my Father, Humphrey B. Neill
The Vermont Ruminator and Father of the Theory of
Contrary Opinion
By Albert R. Neill

Thinking Vermonters "ruminate." Like a cow chewing her cud, the Vermonter turns thoughts over and over in his or her mind, not rushing to judgment. Can this be translated into an investment philosophy? My father published a series of essays on his ruminations of the contrary approach to market trends in 1975, now presented in a revised edition of his publication popular among thinking investors, *The Ruminator*.

My father never attained the riches that he advised others to attain, but he lived a comfortable life, providing for his family. He was conservative in his views (a traditionalist believing in small government, fiscal responsibility, a balanced budget and a laissez faire approach to economics), yet he was progressive in making choices in life and in forging new and creative ways to think and act in the world around him, and in discourse and writing. He pursued vigorously and enthusiastically his interests in books, history, human events, photography (both as an award-winning amateur and professional), the country life in Vermont, and even a short stint as a chicken farmer.

He was a patriot and firmly defended the tenets of American democracy, individualism, and a free market economy. At the age of 21 he joined the Army and served in the last horse-drawn artillery unit under General John J. (Blackjack) Pershing that chased Pancho Villa back into Mexico in the ill-fated Mexican Campaign, and then later in the American Expeditionary Force in France in WW I, where he received a field commission to 2nd lieutenant. On December 7, 1941 he sent a telegram to Secretary of War Stimson volunteering his services to fight the Axis. Too old for active service, he worked energetically on the home front in World War II selling war bonds and served as our county's chairman.

Recently, rummaging through my father's papers I came across a time-faded file with the notation: "Notes – Rough Drafts of Possible Autobio." Inside there was a roughly typed manuscript entitled *Introductory – Chapter I: Through 45 Years of Contrary Opinion,* written about 1975, a year or two before his death in June, 1977. He wrote: "I became imbued with the spirit and practicality of 'contrary opinion' in 1929. It was a wildly fluctuating time in the stock market all year, climaxed by a smashing end of America's most expansive speculative era to that time." At that time, he recounts he was serving as business manager of a division of Brookmire Economic Service* which led him into writing which "might be tagged a financial philosophy," and started a small house organ for Brookmire, entitled, *If, As and When.* It quickly took on the sub-title of *Passing Thoughts and Reflections on Human Nature in Finance.* He notes that this was a writing activity that continued some 45 years to that very day (in 1975).

---

* Brookmire was a large nationally recognized firm specializing in economic and financial research and advisory services. I recall my father telling me that in 1929 Brookmire occupied two full floors of a mid-town office building in Manhattan. By 1932 it had dwindled to one small office in the corner of one floor.

My father cut his teeth in Wall Street in the 1920s with various market advisory services which followed the market daily, researched stocks and offered recommendations for clients. He later moved his office to our home in Larchmont where he maintained a huge wall chart that stretched around three sides of his large 3rd floor studio where he plotted daily the high, low and close of the Dow Jones Averages—industrials, utilities and transportation.

He called himself a "point and figure man," and with his intimate knowledge of market movements put himself in the position to author a well-received volume, *Tape Reading and Market Tactics* (1931). Yet even in these pages you can detect his leanings toward what later became his basis for the Theory of Contrary Opinion: the realization that the stock market is essentially a stage for human interaction, and prices are established by human decision-making as much as by technical indicators.

Then came the Crash and the Great Depression and Humphrey's studies of the human element and crowd psychology led him to formulate the Theory of Contrary Opinion. As the decade of the thirties came to a close, our family moved to Vermont to occupy a spacious 16-room homestead on the outskirts of the village of Saxtons River that had been in the family since 1828. My dad was the fourth generation in the same home, and now I am the fifth. Following, for some 30 years he wrote and published the *Neill Letters of Contrary Opinion* from his vantage point in "contrary country," Vermont. (In the early years the letter was mimeographed, and then later reproduced on an offset printing press. During those mimeograph years, I can recall witnessing my father roll a stencil into his Royal Standard typewriter and type the first and final copy to mount on the mimeograph drum: clearly he had been ruminating about what he had to say for some time before this exercise.) In 1954 he published a small book which attained widespread circulation (including an edition in Japanese), *The Art of Contrary Thinking* (Caxton Press). In 1975 he produced *The Ruminator: A Collection of Thoughts and Suggestions on Contrary Thinking*. Both books are now being re-released by Caxton Press in entirely new and updated 21st Century editions, and in "e-book" formats, including these musings about the original author and an extensive Introduction reflecting on the historical significance of The Theory of Contrary Opinion, and relating these musings to current trends and developments in the marketplace by Tim Vanech, Investment Advisor.

Along the way, the theory of contrary opinion and its author gained public notoriety in a number of ways. In the May 25, 1959 issue, *Time* magazine featured an article on Nicolas Darvas, a Hungarian-born professional dancer, entitled *Pas de Dough* explaining how he had amassed a fortune of over $2,000,000 in the stock market while continuing his dancing career. Among other items of interest, Darvas studied the market backstage between his appearances and was quoted as saying there were two books that he re-read each week, one of them being Humphrey Neill's *Tape Reading and Market Tactics*. The book was then out-of-print and prices shot up for the few copies in the second-hand book market. My father contacted the publisher, B. C. Forbes, who was not in a position to rush out a new edition, but kindly gave the rights to my father and had their office staff type the entire text on mimeograph stencils. My father then issued a "special edition" in mimeographed form with an updated foreword and worksheets for use by the reader and marketed it through his newsletter and limited advertising. Two copies remain in our Vermont library today. On the copyright page he passed on this note of sagacity:

> A requisite for a successful speculator is a 'money mind' … those of us without this tantalizing quality of mind will have to be satisfied with a more gradual accumulation   of   a   share   of   this   world's goods, and be content with making friends, enjoying the   beauties of life and reading books for pleasure and erudition.

And while no records seem to exist, he wrote in a scrapbook carefully kept by my mother, "We sold thousands of these."

In 1967, Edward Johnson II, founder of Fidelity Investments, launched the *Contrafund*, naming it after my father. On the 10th anniversary of the fund in the May 20, 1977 edition of the *Wall Street Journal*, Fidelity ran an ad featuring a photo of my father deep in thought with a young man alongside who queried, "Mr. Neill, on behalf of Fidelity I'd like to acknowledge your theories that led to the development of *Contrafund*. But tell us, sir, what have you been up to lately?" To whom my father replied: "Ruminating, young man, ruminating." Yes, the *Contrafund* was targeted at investors who wanted to benefit from carefully examined contra trends utilized to identify undervalued stocks and, if you will, managers that "ruminated" before making investment decisions. Today, the *Contrafund* has over $60Bn in assets.

In his later years, my dad's eyesight started to fail. I bought him a magnifying light so he could continue to read. Then I flew off to Greece for a long-term work assignment. He purchased a typewriter with jumbo letters (about font size 30 on our computers today). The last note I received from him the letters ran right off the page, so frustrating for a man of letters, who contributed with passion to the market's lexicon—words like "contrary," "ruminate" and others. He passed away shortly after that. On June 6, 1977 he attended a meeting of the public library board of trustees, came home, had supper and fell into an eternal sleep in his favorite chair in the living room. He was 82 years old. On cold winter nights in the old homestead in my imagination I can still hear the *tap, tap, tap* of his Royal Standard as he interprets the day's events from a contrary point-of-view.

Saxtons River, Vermont
May 2010